NEW CLASSICISTS

DINYAR S. WADIA

WADIA ASSOCIATES

Residential Architecture of Distinction

NEW CLASSICISTS

DINYAR S. WADIA

WADIA ASSOCIATES

Residential Architecture of Distinction

FOREWORD BY
H.R.H. THE PRINCE OF WALES

INTRODUCTION BY
PAUL GUNTHER

PRINCIPAL PHOTOGRAPHY BY
JONATHAN WALLEN

DESIGNED & EDITED BY
PHILLIP JAMES DODD

images
Publishing

Dedicated to Gool, my love and soul mate
on this great journey.

Published in Australia in 2007 by
The Images Publishing Group Pty Ltd
ABN 89 059 734 431
6 Bastow Place, Mulgrave, Victoria 3170, Australia
Tel: +61 3 9561 5544 Fax: +61 3 9561 4860
books@images.com.au
www.imagespublishing.com

Copyright © The Images Publishing Group Pty Ltd 2007
The Images Publishing Group Reference Number: 725

National Library of Australia Cataloguing-in-Publication entry:

Dinyar S. Wadia, Wadia Associates: Residential architecture of distinction.

ISBN 978 186470 233 0 (hbk.).

1. Wadia, Dinyar S. 2. Wadia Associates (Firm). 3. Interior decorators – United
States. 4. Interior decoration firms – United States. 5. Architecture, Domestic –
United States – 20th century – Pictorial works. 6. Interior decoration – United
States – 20th century – Pictorial works. I. Dodd, Phillip James. II. Title.
(Series: New classicists).

720.92

Coordinating editor: Robyn Beaver

Production by The Graphic Image Studio Pty Ltd, Mulgrave, Australia
www.tgis.com.au

Digital production by Splitting Image Colour Studio Pty Ltd, Australia
Printed by Everbest Printing Co. Ltd, in Hong Kong/China

Front cover: *A Queen Anne style home on Long Island Sound (see pages 36–51).*
Back cover: *A Georgian style pool house (see pages 72–95).*
Page 1: *An English country cottage (see pages 52–71).*
Page 5: *Detail of a window (see pages 52–71).*
Page 256: *A pergola overlooking formal gardens (see pages 124–145).*

Additional photography

Robert Butscher: *Pages 217, 219*
Farzan Saleem: *Pages 14, 99, 209, 250 (top left)*
Durstan Saylor: *Front cover, pages 10, 36, 37, 38–39, 41, 46, 47, 48, 49,*
51, 168, 169, 171, 172, 173
David Sloane: *Pages 20, 104, 208, 211, 212, 213, 214, 215*
Steve Turner: *Page 45*
Dinyar Wadia: *Pages 16, 17, 210, 220, 221*

"THOU ART THE SKY and thou art the nest as well.
O beautiful, there in the nest it is thy love that encloses the soul with colors and sounds and scents.
There comes the morning with the golden basket in her right hand bearing the wreath of beauty,
Silently to crown the earth …"

Rabindranath Tagore

The entrance façade of an American Shingle style home (see pages 110–123).

CONTENTS

WADIA ASSOCIATES
RESIDENTIAL ARCHITECTURE OF DISTINCTION

CLARENCE HOUSE

It is always a great pleasure to hear from the alumni of my former Institute for Architecture and I was delighted when a previous student wrote with details of a firm he now works for in Connecticut – Wadia Associates.

Browsing the portfolio enclosed, I was immediately struck by the way that this practice commands such a broad range of architectural language, creating buildings for the 21st Century that draw unabashed from the living traditions of architecture, be they classical, gothic or vernacular. It came as no surprise to discover that Dinyar Wadia is a native of Bombay and cites the wealth and diversity of architectural styles in that city as a formative influence. I have made no secret of my own belief that it is by opening our eyes to the design of the past, as he so clearly does, we are best equipped to satisfy the contemporary brief. The value of the buildings presented in these pages is clear – their confident elevations, high and pleasant light-filled rooms, the harmonious relationship fostered between house and landscape. Dinyar also clearly relishes his command of architectural languages whose enduring appeal guarantees a commission continues to be enjoyed long after prevailing fashions have moved on. The broad variety of these designs also evidences a will to listen to the client, producing a solution crafted to their needs rather than imposed upon them…

All considered, it is a delight to note that Wadia Associates continues to thrive and grow, producing work whose charm and self-effacement needs no sham advertising or bogus claims of innovation that must have bewitched commissioners of the self consciously "modern".

While this portfolio details private houses and associated structures in the tradition of the Great Estates, I hope it will serve as an inspiration to those who are crafting our new neighbourhoods, towns and cities not only in the States, but around the world, giving a broader audience the opportunity to experience daily the benefits of living, timeless traditions in our built environment.

The porch extends this Queen Anne style home into the landscape (see pages 36–51).

INTRODUCTION

By

Paul Gunther

President

The Institute of Classical Architecture & Classical America

WHEN, AT THE DAWN OF THE 21ST CENTURY, the connoisseur, student, or practitioner of design contemplates New England and in particular its verdant and vibrant southwestern region in Fairfield County, Connecticut, he or she might think concurrently of two much-publicized trends: an unprecedented appreciation of mid 20th-century modernist achievement; and the great size, opulence and quality of great estates, built by our nation's financial giants and barons of industry.

On the modernist front, the now-fabled achievements of American pioneers are becoming preserved artifacts of architectural history and a quickly fading measure of rupture with the past. Philip Johnson's Glass House (1949) or Paul Rudolph and his Art and Architecture Building for Yale University (1963) stand out as world-renowned cases in point. The 20th-century preservationists, unified by an international advocacy group called DOCOMOMO, are in part responsible for such growing awareness, extending as their work does to all recorded modernist homes located throughout the area. These are carefully documented by local geography as a tool of vigilance and protectionist advocacy. Further evidence comes from W.W. Norton's 2006 publication of *The Harvard Five in New Canaan,* which explores how those at America's first architecture school to embrace the Bauhaus, at the expense of the Beaux-Arts, made their then-revolutionary practices locally manifest. Attention is thus being paid in essence to the newest old houses.

The second local trend reverberates with a much older built distinction reflected in the industry and geographical felicitousness of the Constitution State's alluring topography, beckoning those well-served by the economic juggernaut of nearby and well-connected New York City. What distinguished Connecticut's formation from the rest of colonial America was above all the binding social and communitarian contract of the town as a defining political and geographical division. The arrival of trains from New York City in the latter half of the 19th century heralded the arrival of affluent commuters escaping the summer heat. Many soon decided to set up permanent residence, building homes that reflected their newfound financial and social status within the community. The historic development pattern of Greenwich, New Canaan, and their neighboring towns and villages was thus set in motion—as it continues today. Indeed this new century's early years have brought a new wave of residents who, like so many of their predecessors, have both the will and means to grace the bucolic wooded landscape with traditional design solutions augmented with a full-throttled embrace of contemporary construction methods, new materials, and the expected amenities of modern life.

So as the trail-blazing, yet aging exemplars of modernism themselves come to define and inform what is now just one more aspect of American architectural tradition, the time is right—and the arguments stronger than ever—to come full circle and advance further a reborn appreciation of classicism and its practice today in Connecticut and across the nation.

Classicism and its varied vernacular interpretations constitute a comparable—if more time-tested—living cultural force whose continual reinvention and adaptation appeal anew across a broad range of clients, from those seeking a new or renewed home to those charged with planning entire communities or commercial centers. Indeed, this new classicism represents a potent architectural phenomenon, which a new century heralds and to which attention must now be paid.

The forecourt façade of a French Country home (see pages 122–143).

Historicizing focus on more recent architectural precedents, deemed worthy of study and emulation by many design professionals, likewise lends fresh currency to Kenyon Cox's observation in his seminal book *The Classic Point of View*, "Wherever, in modern art as in the art of the past, you find an artist of real power of design—and we have had such—you find the note of classicism, of respect for tradition, of connection with everything fine and noble that has gone before." In sum, the lessons of history, and the cultural memory enlivening them throughout its record, must serve as a resource for meeting design challenges of the present day. Denial of this credo is no longer viable or pertinent; renouncement of classicism in opposition to the last century's construct of modernism has ceased to frame a meaningful debate; *the question of style* has yielded instead to the pursuit of excellence in meeting diverse contemporary preferences and needs. For many clients, novelty as a satisfactory (let alone revolutionary) end in itself holds little currency today.

This new appreciation of tradition's full force heralds this insightful exploration of the design intelligence characterizing the prodigious, ongoing career of Dinyar Wadia and his New Canaan-based practice. Since 1975, his contemporary application of classical forms and their varying means of expression have helped ensure the region's historic continuum as expressed through the communities and the residences defining them. Although not limited to New Canaan as this volume reveals, Wadia's home base serves well as a defining geographic locus typifying the landscape, political divisions, and traditions of its surrounding region.

I welcome Wadia's pluralistic example to the *New Classicists* series as an instructive guide for all those who, whether as client or practitioner, share his well-proven pursuit of beauty unrestrained by any preconceived, polemical, or hierarchical notions of style. Ranging from Tudor to Georgian, from Colonial Revival to French

Renaissance, the firm's focus has been on the meeting of client needs and lifestyle through a refined, original, and always flexible examination of prospective design solutions that interpret differing facets of the Classical tradition. The results are not only fine individual structures, but also stronger neighborhoods and built landscapes respectful of past excellence, which demonstrate reinvention and renewal. And the firm's robust embrace of new technologies and materials, which together redefine affordable, sustainable, and environmentally sound options, has kept its creative arsenal fully at the design forefront.

The architect and historian J. Frederick Kelly wrote in his still-definitive 1924 volume, *Early Domestic Architecture of Connecticut*, "The early Connecticut house was a new creation, wherein the use of materials and the manner of construction were largely the result of

Old World tradition, modified to meet an entirely new and different set of conditions." Such principles endure in the work this volume reveals. And just as Kelly relayed the very earliest colonial architecture of the state for study and appreciation, so can the Wadia example steer future practitioners of any locale who look to the best lessons of the past in shaping the future.

The New Classicists series of monographs featuring the work of contemporary American practitioners complements, among other resources, the Institute's *Classical America Series in Art and Architecture*, which for thirty years has been under the determined watch and frequent contributing authorship of Henry Hope Reed and his scholarly colleagues. Such publications simultaneously reflect and extend a broad-based and ongoing rediscovery of classicism. Future excellence requires by definition an understanding of precedent and such books play a central pedagogical role accordingly. The classicist dares, in the words of Isaac Newton, to "stand on the shoulders of giants;" these volumes, like the structures they record, make it possible for such continuity to remain in lively force. The design solutions revealed lie not in slavish imitation but in a search for guiding excellence in both detail and overall conception; they lie in the exacting application of past models to the present day. Such a guiding principle should be the hallmark of classicists as it is of latter-day modernists; all must discover and practice likewise if they are to succeed in creating anew.

In the following pages, the reader can examine the work of Dinyar Wadia and how his eponymous firm has kept alive a tradition of place and of continuing reinvention. On behalf of the Institute of Classical Architecture & Classical America, of which Dinyar Wadia is a generous member and leading inspiration, I commend his example and thank him for it.

Paul Gunther

An addition to a historic John Russell Pope house in Watch Hill, Rhode Island (see pages 200–207).

Paul Gunther is the President of the Institute of Classical Architecture & Classical America—a national educational and advocacy organization dedicated to the Classical design vocabulary in architecture and its allied arts. Before his appointment in 2003, Paul served as Vice President of Institutional Advancement and Director of Development at the New York Historical Society. He has also worked extensively with The American Center in Paris, and The Municipal Art Society.

Dinyar Wadia, with his two rough collies Arjun and Draupadi.

DINYAR S. WADIA

A Classical Journey

By

Suzanne Knutson

SINCE FOUNDING WADIA ASSOCIATES in New Canaan, Connecticut, more than 30 years ago, Dinyar Wadia has developed a well-earned reputation for designing and constructing finely detailed, traditionally styled homes for discriminating clients. Although he counts numerous projects nationwide, Wadia is best known for the elegant residences he has designed and constructed within the exclusive confines of Fairfield County. This relatively small corner of southwestern Connecticut has long been a mecca for the well-to-do who are drawn by the region's sparkling views of Long Island Sound, the lush beauty of its back country, and its proximity to New York City.

During the Great Estates era, which began in the late 19th century and continued until World War II, those at the forefront of American business and industry began to build country estates in this region as logical extensions of their prosperity. Some designed simple and informally furnished summer homes. Others, not satisfied with mere comfort, built homes that ultimately became a testament to their wealth and power. Unfettered by financial constraints, the owners expressed their individuality through the design of their homes. Medieval castles, Italian villas, French châteaux and English manor houses vied for attention as the estate builders searched for designs that reflected their tastes and interests. Although the Great Estates era is now but a faint memory, its legacy remains in the diversity of architectural styles to be found in this region.

It has been Wadia's challenge over these many years to carefully navigate within this eclectic framework of architectural styles to create beautiful, livable designs that are contemporary in the modern world, yet remain respectful of traditional classical design. Along the way, he has built a thriving design practice that is as likely to be working on a new design as it is reinventing and renovating one of Fairfield County's grand old estates. In a region where wealth often manifests itself in lavish ostentation, Wadia has been a pillar of distinctive and subdued elegance. With a refined taste and dignified presence, Wadia's homes are grand yet effortlessly gracious, casual yet elegant.

Wadia developed his love of architecture and unerring eye for distinction as a child growing up in Bombay, India. His mother came from a family of builders so it was only natural that he would develop a keen interest in the rich architecture of his native city. With its infrastructure of huge squares and arcades connecting one part of the city to another, Bombay offered a sophisticated education in city planning and organization. The Gateway of India, a mere stone's throw from his childhood home, gave Wadia an appreciation for the use of masonry as an essential building material. And the magnificent public buildings erected by the British during their colonization of India—from the Bombay Zoo to the Opera House to the Municipal Library—provided him with an enviable introduction to traditional architecture. One of his favorite structures was Victoria Terminus, India's extraordinary railway station, which combines an ornate mixture of Hindu and Gothic architecture. It doesn't take a trained eye to marvel at how hard the British worked to make it seem like a domestic structure.

There were lessons to be learned outside the city's limits as well. During the summer, Wadia would vacation outside Bombay in a wonderful house his mother inherited. It was from this house, which was surrounded by lush gardens, waterfalls, and gazebos, that Wadia first gained an appreciation for the intimate relationship between building structures and their surrounding landscape, an appreciation that would form the core of his design philosophy later on in his career.

Wadia's family home in Bombay is a blend of Indian and Western architectural elements.

Given these early influences, it was only natural that Wadia would pursue a degree in architecture. After completing a five-year program at the Maharaja Sayajirao University of Baroda in India, a curriculum that included a year's study of fine arts and several courses in landscape architecture, Wadia met and married his wife, Gool. For two years they lived in Bombay while Wadia worked as an architect. But it was hard to get a good job without a master's degree, and Wadia had loftier ambitions. He was also growing increasingly disenchanted with the political climate in India. Although it had a very strong free press, the Indian democracy at the time didn't afford its citizens the same type of freedom that Americans take for granted.

Lured by big skyscrapers and the excitement of New York City, Wadia departed from his home country and enrolled at Columbia University in 1968 to study for a graduate degree in architecture. After graduating as a William Kinney Fellow, Wadia received two very attractive job offers. The first was an offer to work for one of his professors, Victor Christ-Janer, at his architectural firm in New Canaan, Connecticut. Although the office was small, the job would give him an opportunity to participate in the project design process from start to finish. The second offer was from a very large, prestigious firm in New York City. It had a huge office in Manhattan, which churned out drawings for other architectural firms. Although the prospect of working in the city was very exciting and the Manhattan firm offered a salary of 25 cents more per hour (not an insignificant amount of money at the time), Wadia was concerned that the work seemed very compartmentalized. He worried that he would be drawing stair details for the rest of his life. After much soul

searching, he ultimately decided to take the job in New Canaan, a decision he's grateful for to this day. Thankfully, there was no compartmentalizing. He worked on assignments from inception to completion, including construction management. Overall, it was a rewarding experience, one that Wadia credits with rounding out his professional skills. Perhaps as importantly, it was from Christ-Janer that Wadia learned two very valuable professional lessons. The first was the importance of really listening to people, and the second was the understanding that ego has no place in successful design.

Under Christ-Janer's tutelage, Wadia began his career in the modern vernacular. Coincidentally, the firm was based in New Canaan, the same town made famous by Philip Johnson and his glass-walled house. The circumstances were perfect for a career in modern architecture, and for six years that's how Wadia honed his craft. Yet, while his skill grew impressively, he found his inspiration waning. Wadia found himself drawn instead to the beauty and charm of the traditional buildings in New Canaan and the surrounding towns of Fairfield County. The scale of the structures and their elegant detailing awoke a passion for classical design that was first expressed in his native India. Determined to heed his passion, Wadia decided to strike out on his own in 1975 to design traditionally inspired homes.

Like other architects of his generation, Wadia is largely self-taught in classical and traditional design. Although the Columbia campus is replete with historic buildings and a library boasting the most significant collection of architectural texts in America, classical design had fallen out of favor by his time there and was excluded from the curriculum in favor of a modern aesthetic. For guidance in classical design, Wadia instead relied upon the training he received in India

Located in New Canaan, the Wiley house was designed by Philip Johnson in 1953, and recently renovated by Wadia.

and drew inspiration from the magnificent buildings that infused the memories of his childhood. Particularly helpful were the measured drawings of buildings he had surveyed as a student—structures that spanned a wide variety of periods and styles including Indian, Dutch, Portuguese, French, and English Colonial architecture. In addition, as part of his studies, Wadia was required to read *A History of Architecture* by Sir Banister Fletcher, widely considered to be the bible of architectural history and which ultimately proved to be an invaluable source to him on the principles of classicism. Wadia was also a great admirer of the work of the renowned architects John Russell Pope, Sir Edwin Lutyens, and Stanford White, all of whom he credits with having had a profound impact on his own design philosophy.

Rather than specialize in a single type of design, Wadia's business philosophy has always been to excel at all traditional styles of architecture. Over the past thirty years, he has demonstrated a remarkable versatility and adaptability with projects ranging from, for example, a Colonial Revival farmhouse to a French Normandy château; a Georgian style mansion to a quaint English country potting shed; or an informal American Shingle style home to a Tudor manor house. Regardless of the architectural style, Wadia's design philosophy emphasizes a strict attention to detail, exceptional workmanship, the use of luxurious materials, and the integral relationship between a house and its surrounding landscape.

An avowed garden-lover, Wadia has traveled extensively to visit the world's finest gardens. He has been quoted as saying, "A house without a garden has no soul," and in fact, he has developed a well-deserved reputation for building homes that seem rooted in the landscape. Rather than indiscriminately tear down trees to facilitate the construction phase of a project, Wadia takes pains to site each residence so that it is nestled naturally into the surrounding landscape. Likewise, he goes to great lengths to ensure that windows are positioned to their best advantage to capture natural light and look out over a special view. If there is a single theme that characterizes all of his projects, it is that his homes seem to wrap themselves around the garden in an artful embrace.

Although he is loyal to a classical aesthetic, Wadia nonetheless has been able to bridge the divide between the traditional and the modern by designing homes of timeless beauty that also incorporate modern amenities to meet the contemporary needs of his clients. One of his greatest challenges has been to accommodate new room types within a classical framework. While his residences feature the classic proportions of traditional architecture, Wadia is creative when it comes to room usage, often reinventing interior spaces to include family–breakfast–kitchen combinations, exercise rooms and spas, and

The Gateway of India, in Bombay, was built in 1924 to commemorate a visit by the Prince of Wales.

extensive master bath areas. Of course, such rooms were unheard of in the traditional vernacular, but Wadia is respectful of the desires of his clients and their need for a home that is practical and livable, as well as beautiful.

Together with his design team—which consists of eight architectural designers, an interior decorator, several construction managers, and numerous support staff—Wadia has been successful in reinterpreting the past and updating it for the present. Little did he know that the classical journey he embarked upon as a young man would one day result in such a busy and rewarding practice, proof that the timeless beauty of traditional design will always be appreciated. It is his hope that future generations of architects will be inspired by the images contained in this book and will continue the journey he began all those years ago.

An example of the symbiotic relationship between a Wadia-designed home and its gardens (see pages 124–145).

SELECTED WORKS

Our Growing Portfolio

WADIA ASSOCIATES
RESIDENTIAL ARCHITECTURE OF DISTINCTION

OLD MEETS NEW DISCREETLY

New Canaan, Connecticut

BUILT IN 1929 DURING THE GREAT ESTATES ERA, this brick and limestone country estate is a wonderful example of architecture in the grand manner. It was designed by New York architect William B. Tubby, who rose to prominence during this period for his outstanding designs that included Waveny House in New Canaan, Dunnellen Hall in Greenwich, and the Greenwich Library. Yet for all its beauty and gracious bearing, the current owners of the home felt that it lacked sufficient living space for the family to gather comfortably together. Their request for an addition posed the unique design challenge of expanding the square footage of the house without making it seem larger than its already sizeable dimensions.

To preserve the architectural integrity of the house, Wadia left the original house intact, opting instead to tuck a new wing onto the back of the house, discreetly out of sight from the entry approach. To ensure a seamless transition between the old and the new, the Indiana limestone used on the exterior of the house was power ground to give it the same texture and patina as the existing stone.

Ultimately, the addition included a new kitchen, great room, outdoor courtyard, and a playroom. Providing the inspiration for the great room was Castle Duart, located on the Isle of Mull, and featured in the 1999 movie *Entrapment* in which Sean Connery and Catherine Zeta-Jones, playing art thieves, practice their moves for a high-tech heist. Smitten by the stylish setting, the clients asked Wadia to recreate a similar sort of room for their new addition, a request he relished. Featuring a double-height ceiling, massive stone fireplace with intricate carvings, and custom bronze handrails leading up to a second-story mezzanine, the great room has become a treasured place for the family to gather. Linking this room to the main residence is a glass-paned corridor featuring iron frames and true divided lights. Stunning views of the garden terrace are on display on one side, while the new kitchen is visible through the courtyard, which flanks the other side of the corridor. Together with the roof lights in the kitchen and double-height bay windows in the great room, the new space is drenched in sunlight, inviting the family to linger in its welcoming glow.

Opposite: *The entrance façade of the existing house.*

Above: *Overlooking the mature gardens, the new great room is sited to complement the architecture of the existing house.*

GARDEN FACADE

The great room overlooks the formal gardens, and is connected to the main house by a window-clad gallery topped with brick crenelations.

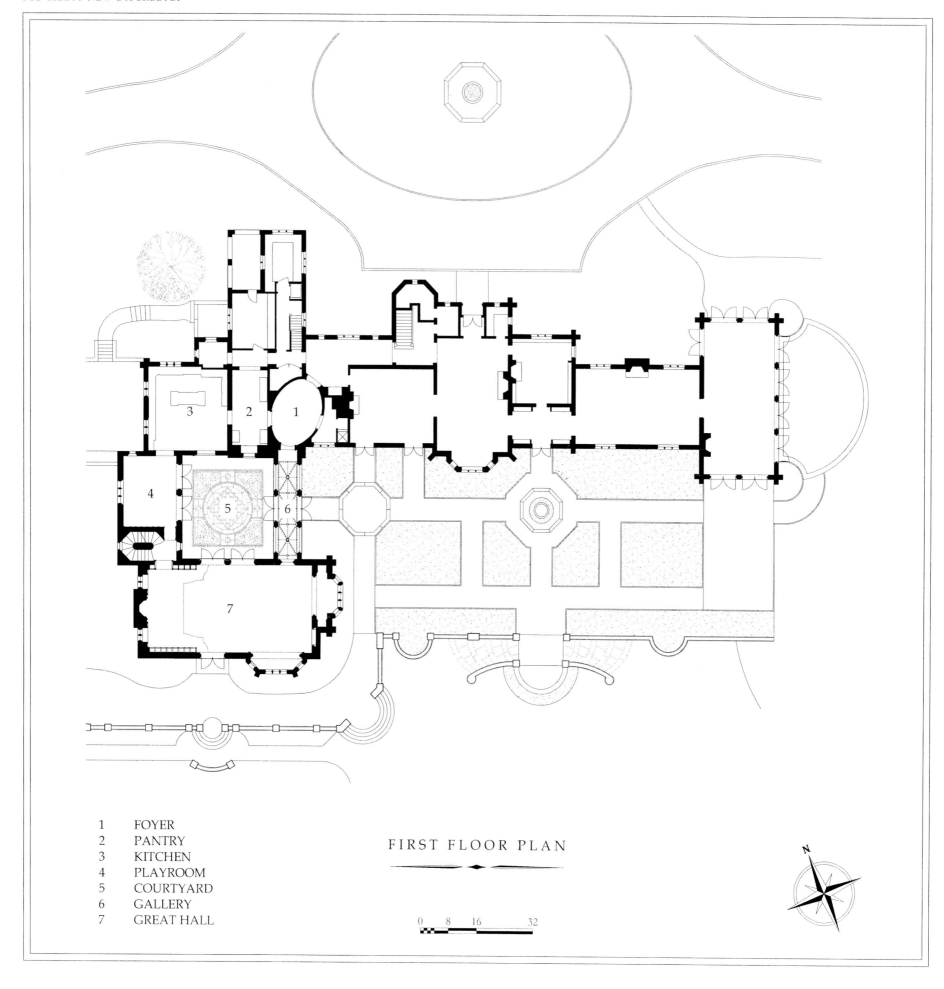

1 FOYER
2 PANTRY
3 KITCHEN
4 PLAYROOM
5 COURTYARD
6 GALLERY
7 GREAT HALL

FIRST FLOOR PLAN

0 8 16   32

Looking through the outdoor courtyard to the kitchen beyond.

The dramatic space of the great room is the focal point of the new wing.

Hand-carved Elizabethan details are incorporated into the interior stonework that frames the bay windows in the great room.

The study area is drenched in sunlight and offers views of the garden terrace and formal gardens.

The library features custom-designed walnut bookcases, with Gothic arches and dropped finials.

This existing fireplace was extensively restored, with much of the wood paneling and carving completely replaced.

The imposing fireplace in the library is hand-carved from limestone and ornamented with Elizabethan motifs.

The glass-paned corridor that connects the main house to the great room beyond features a series of stone groin vaults.

The oval foyer, connecting through to the kitchen, is embellished with a decorative wainscot and ceiling crown.

The kitchen features custom-designed oak cabinets, designed to resemble pieces of individual furniture.

A skylight and ample windows flood the kitchen with natural light.

QUEEN ANNE SPLENDOR
ON LONG ISLAND SOUND

Greenwich, Connecticut

FRAMED BETWEEN HUGE OAK TREES, this Queen Anne home built in the late 19th century unveils its treasures in tantalizing fashion. As one approaches the house from the driveway, a sense of intrigue begins to build as the house comes into view, nestled gracefully within the mature landscape. The full extent of its splendor isn't fully revealed, however, until one enters the house and comes face to face with the stunning view of Long Island Sound, an extraordinary axial vista that is on display through oversized windows gracing each of the rooms facing the water. A mere stone's throw from the Belle Haven Yacht Club in Greenwich, the house has the great good fortune of sitting on a peninsula jutting out into the surrounding water. This is, unquestionably, drama at its best.

Given how seamlessly the house seems to rise from its surroundings, it is hard to imagine that it was extensively gutted and renovated by Wadia and his design team little more than a decade ago. Except for the living room and portions of the front façade, most of the rest of the home is newly constructed.

The house is designed to be deliberately asymmetrical. Anchoring one end of the front of the house is a circular tower enclosing the main entrance on the first floor and a wonderfully intimate reading room on the second floor. The other end of the front façade features a projecting gable with oriel windows set above the living room's ornately detailed leaded glass windows, which were restored during the renovation. Inspired by the owner's visit to the Doge's Palace in Venice, Wadia incorporated a three-arch motif in the master bedroom, complete with an old-fashioned sleeping porch and sliding glass pocket windows that lend the room a delightfully exotic touch.

Each of the rooms facing the water was designed with the stunning view in mind. In a concession to the extraordinary setting, Wadia incorporated large sheets of glass into the design, rather than more traditional windows divided by panes, to ensure an unobstructed view of the water. In addition, generously proportioned verandas wrapping around the side and rear of the house offer cozy spots for breakfast or tea and irresistible views of the rising and setting sun.

Opposite: *The front façade at dusk.*

Above: *The porches of the house are located to provide spectacular views of the shoreline.*

PARTIAL
BACK ELEVATION

Previous pages: *A panoramic view of the house as seen from Long Island Sound.*

Above: *Typical of Queen Anne style homes, the waterfront façade features a variety of architectural elements.*

The new waterfront pavilion.

One of the many porches that provide views of the gardens and Long Island Sound beyond.

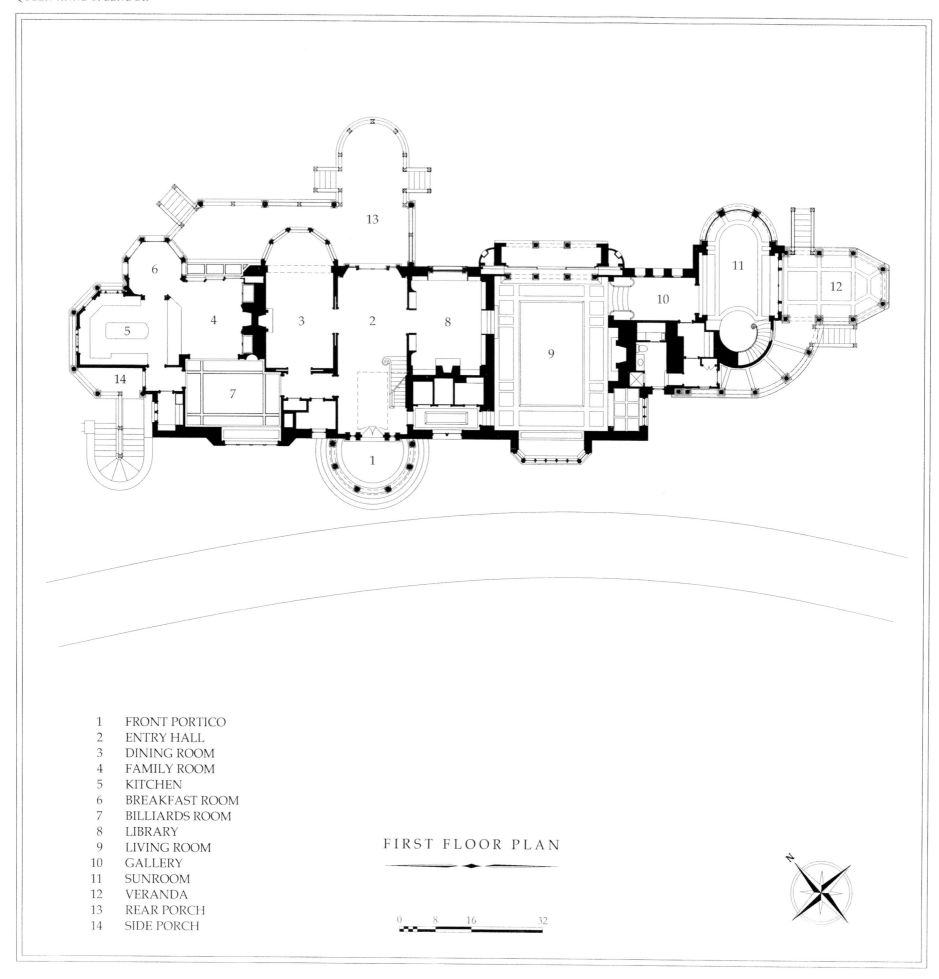

FIRST FLOOR PLAN

1   FRONT PORTICO
2   ENTRY HALL
3   DINING ROOM
4   FAMILY ROOM
5   KITCHEN
6   BREAKFAST ROOM
7   BILLIARDS ROOM
8   LIBRARY
9   LIVING ROOM
10 GALLERY
11 SUNROOM
12 VERANDA
13 REAR PORCH
14 SIDE PORCH

0   8   16   32

An aerial view of the house nestled into the landscape of mature trees.

The entrance hall offers an axial view out onto Long Island Sound.

The circular reading room is located on the landing of the entrance tower.

Detail of the restored stained glass window in the living room.

A view from the library through to the dining room.

The master bedroom opens out to an old-fashioned sleeping porch.

The master bedroom features a three-arched opening, reminiscent of those found in Venice.

GITANJALI

New Canaan, Connecticut

GITANJALI IS AN EPIC POEM OF LOVE AND PRAISE written by the Indian poet laureate Rabindranath Tagore. As the perfect expression of the essence of his home, it is the name Wadia chose for his English country house, a local gem hidden on a quiet road north of the village of New Canaan. It is a true English country setting—a bucolic and pastoral place where rolling meadows and 200-year-old trees still exist. Reflecting Wadia's appreciation for the intimate relationship between building structures and their surrounding landscape, the house and its gardens are symbiotic: the house provides the gardens with a reason for existing, while the gardens shelter the house and extend it outward into the surrounding landscape. Together, they form a private world that reveals itself gradually and unexpectedly.

Gitanjali was originally built in 1870 as the guest cottage of a large estate whose main house was demolished long ago. When Wadia purchased the property in 1998, the house and gardens had been severely neglected, and the magnificent trees—which were planted as mature specimens by the original owners—were choking from poison oak and ivy. Though the house was a wreck, it occupied a nice spot anchored by two huge ash trees. Tearing down the house and rebuilding would have meant cutting down the two trees, an unthinkable act for Wadia, so he decided to renovate and salvage as much as possible. Remarkably, the exterior of the house today looks nearly identical to the original structure, right down to the climbing hydrangea over the front door, which was peeled off the front of the house and supported with scaffolding while workers put up new crossbeams and finished the façade with stucco.

The renovation involved extensive, yet unobtrusive, additions and modifications that borrow from the finest details of the original home. The interior was completely reconfigured to include new bedrooms with baths en suite, a large country kitchen with a sitting area warmed by a large limestone fireplace, and a loggia for summer dining overlooking the magnificent gardens. The end result is an exquisitely detailed "cottage" that is both spacious and modern while retaining the modest charm of the original house. Yet it is the interplay between the house and the gardens outside that lingers in one's memory—just as Wadia intended.

Opposite: *The house viewed from its gardens.*

Above: *The entrance façade.*

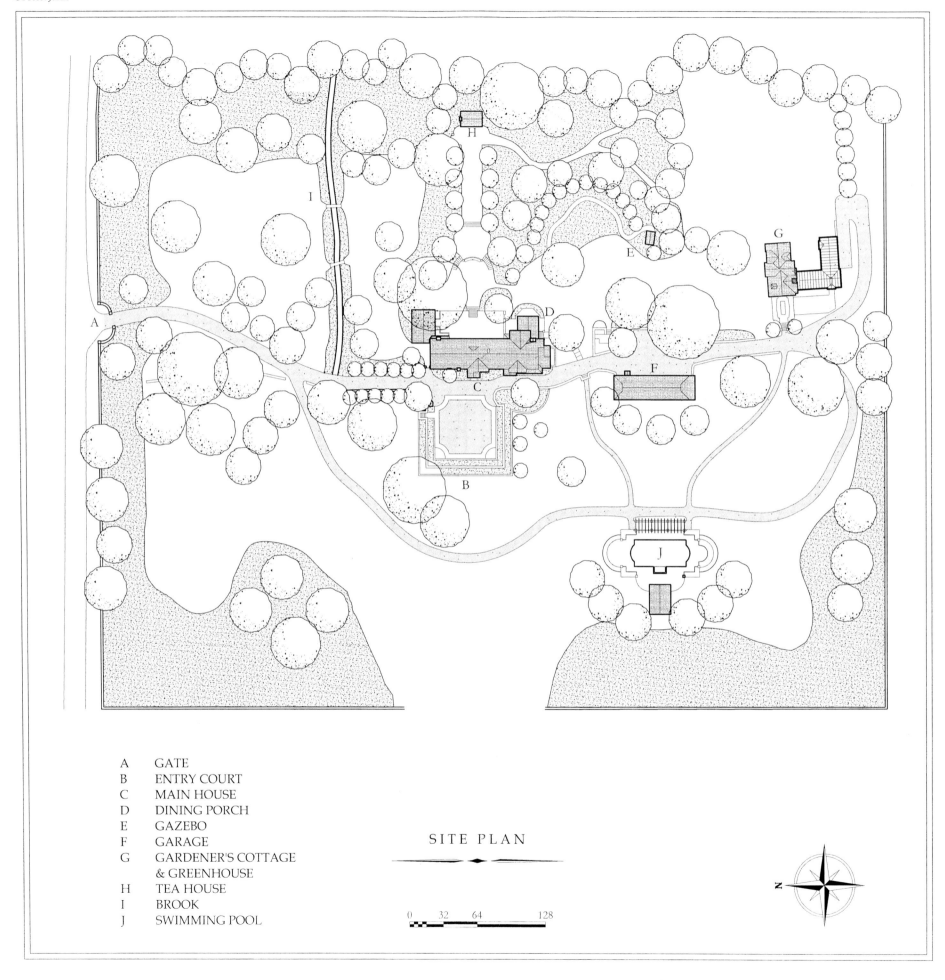

A   GATE
B   ENTRY COURT
C   MAIN HOUSE
D   DINING PORCH
E   GAZEBO
F   GARAGE
G   GARDENER'S COTTAGE
     & GREENHOUSE
H   TEA HOUSE
I   BROOK
J   SWIMMING POOL

SITE PLAN

0   32   64   128

Previous pages: *The dining loggia provides spectacular views of the gardens.*

Above: *In renovating the existing house it was important to retain its old-world charm.*

The Tea House is nestled in the mature gardens.

The Tea House provides a quaint hideaway.

The gardens at Gitanjali.

A doorway provides access to the secret gardens.

Detail of the half-timbering, decorative brackets, and carved roof fascia.

The juxtaposition of gables on the breakfast room façade.

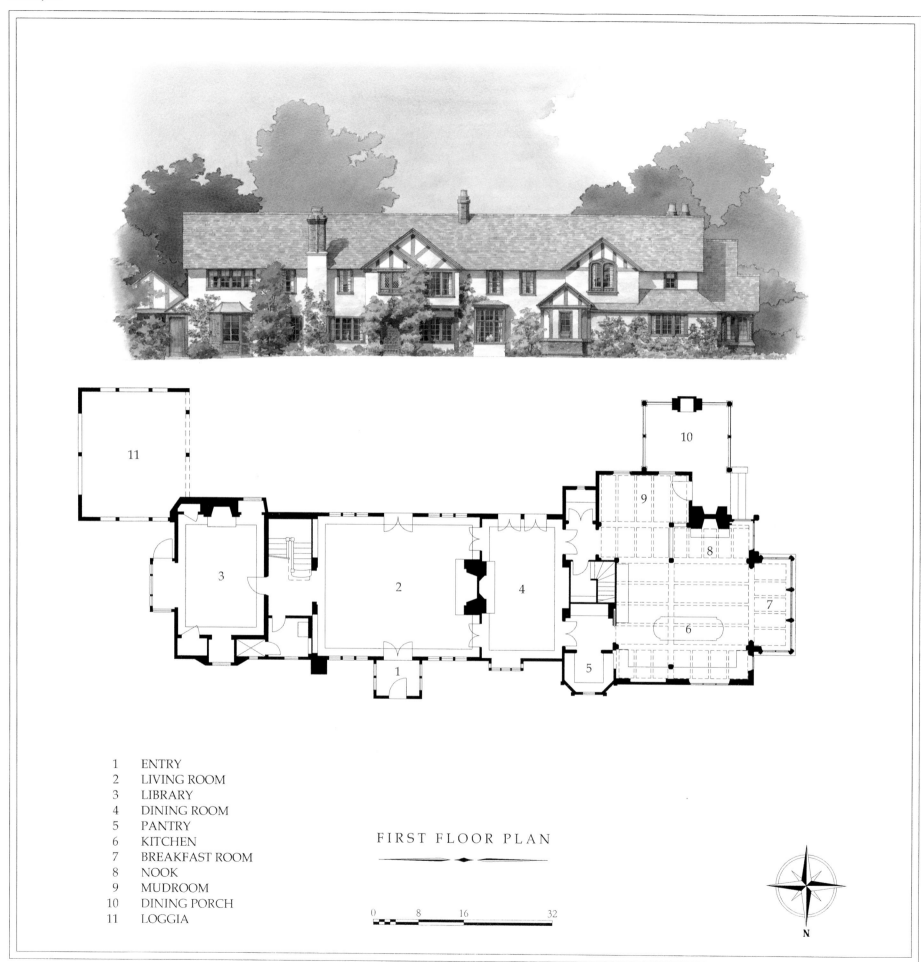

1   ENTRY
2   LIVING ROOM
3   LIBRARY
4   DINING ROOM
5   PANTRY
6   KITCHEN
7   BREAKFAST ROOM
8   NOOK
9   MUDROOM
10   DINING PORCH
11   LOGGIA

FIRST FLOOR PLAN

0   8   16   32

N

The garden façade.

The entrance vestibule features custom-carved oak doors and wainscoting.

The kitchen opens to a cozy sitting area with a limestone fireplace.

The study is paneled in knotty pine and has wide white oak floorboards, both of which add to its old-world charm.

Throughout the house there are views overlooking the spectacular gardens.

Intricate floral carvings are incorporated into the oak millwork.

The second-floor gallery was designed to include custom built-in display cabinets.

A GEORGIAN COUNTRY ESTATE

Greenwich, Connecticut

THE SCENIC BEAUTY OF GREENWICH'S MID-COUNTRY sets the stage for the formal grandeur of this magnificent country estate. The brick and limestone Georgian design was inspired by the owners' preference for something tasteful and conservative on the one hand, yet grand enough to readily accommodate the frequent large-scale entertaining required for the philanthropic and fund-raising work that the family is involved in.

In keeping with traditional Georgian style, the front façade of the house is elegant yet restrained, featuring relatively little ornamentation with the exception of limestone accents for the quoins, window surrounds, and entrance portico. The rear of the house is undeniably grand, with long sweeping views of the lawn and formal garden from the back terrace. Centered between bay windows topped with circular balustrades, the rear portico is proportioned exquisitely, and is given further emphasis by limestone pilasters and columns that continue up to the second floor. The prominence of the portico is enhanced by the entablature, which comprises a single slab of limestone that was so heavy it required special construction equipment to hoist it into place.

The interior of the house is equally as grand. The ample dimensions and luxurious details of the principal rooms bestow upon them an enviable elegance. A cupola above the central staircase leading off the entryway bathes the sweeping stair hall in sunlight. To give the space added distinction, the staircase was custom-designed and the balusters were individually carved from mahogany. In keeping with the formal symmetry of Georgian architecture, the dining room and living room lead off either side of the stair hall. The dining room ceiling features delicate plasterwork in the Adam style. Its intricate ornamentation is painted in soft pastel shades giving it a wonderful balance of formal grandeur and style.

Many of the rooms in the house were fitted with antique stone fireplaces procured from England. Such was the case with the library, which also features custom-made burled oak paneling milled in England. The decorative motifs reflected in the paneling are recurring elements that can be found throughout the architectural design of the house. This continuity is essential to the symmetry of Georgian design, and provides the foundation for the refined elegance associated with this architectural style.

Opposite: *The front façade viewed from the motor court.*

Above: *The rear portico dominates the garden façade.*

Previous pages: *The rear façade of the house overlooks the formal gardens and sweeping lawn.*

Above: *The garden façade includes a second-floor sleeping porch.*

The bay windows, door surrounds, and quoins are all fabricated from Indiana limestone.

The garden loggia is fabricated from limestone and includes Doric columns that complement the Georgian architecture of the house.

The garden porch overlooks the gardens below.

Details showing the use of limestone—at the bay windows, sleeping porch, carved front door surround, and garden portico.

Featuring the same materials and details, the pool house visually connects to the main house.

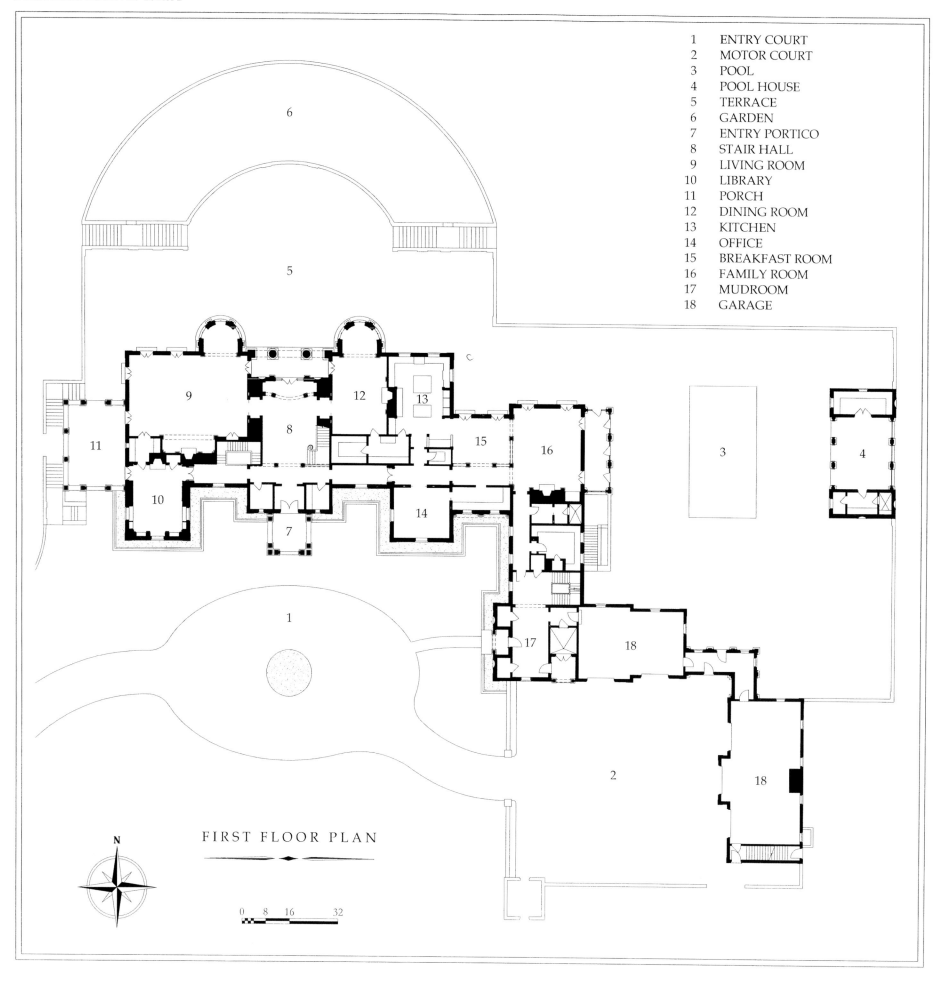

1 ENTRY COURT
2 MOTOR COURT
3 POOL
4 POOL HOUSE
5 TERRACE
6 GARDEN
7 ENTRY PORTICO
8 STAIR HALL
9 LIVING ROOM
10 LIBRARY
11 PORCH
12 DINING ROOM
13 KITCHEN
14 OFFICE
15 BREAKFAST ROOM
16 FAMILY ROOM
17 MUDROOM
18 GARAGE

FIRST FLOOR PLAN

N

0   8   16   32

The paneled entrance vestibule welcomes visitors.

Detail of the custom-designed mahogany staircase. The individual balusters are designed as Doric columns, topped with urns.

The three-story-high stair hall, lit from above by the cupola.

The reading room, with a Palladian opening overlooking the stair hall.

An axial view from the living room through to the dining room.

A design sketch of the dining room's decorative plaster ceiling, inspired by the work of the 18th-century architect, Robert Adam.

The formal dining room features an Adam-esque ceiling, faux-painted marble pilasters, and an antique marble fireplace.

The paneled library was custom-fabricated in England from burled oak.

The library features an antique marble fireplace that was chosen to specifically fit with the architectural motifs that appear in the paneling.

The family room includes built-in cabinets and bookcases.

The second-floor stair landing opens out onto a balcony overlooking the private gardens.

The private sitting room in the master suite.

The master dressing room.

WATERFRONT ELEGANCE
HOME TO A TREASURED COLLECTION

Darien, Connecticut

WHEN THE OWNERS OF THIS HOME approached Wadia about designing a house on a parcel of land they had purchased overlooking Long Island Sound, one of their chief concerns was that it would provide them with an appropriate venue to display their collection of Asian art and collectibles, accumulated during a lengthy stay in Japan. Ultimately, its size and anticipated importance in the interior design of the home left little doubt that this Asian influence should be referenced in the final design of the house.

Reflecting this influence, the house was designed to exude an air of intimacy. The hipped roofs and single-story rooms projecting from the front façade were a deliberate attempt to manipulate the scale of the house. Reminiscent of a pavilion with a cluster of linking structures, the house is built from Mankato Kasota stone from Minnesota, a cream-colored limestone with a cleft face that provides an element of depth and texture to the exterior of the house. Clay tiles for the roof complement the texture and color of the stone, while Indiana limestone offers an appealing contrast for decorative accents.

The rooms in the rear of the house were designed to take full advantage of the water view. A series of French doors topped with transoms open out to the rear terrace, a magnificently crafted space that extends the house into the lovely setting beyond. Balustrades carved from limestone and extra wide steps leading to the formal garden lend a wonderful sense of luxury to the rear façade.

Inside, the owners' art and collectibles are displayed in numerous niches carved into the walls and door openings. The interiors of all the rooms, most of which were decorated by Wadia's design team, feature a subtle elegance designed to complement the impressive display and highlight the beautiful view. Intricate plasterwork adorns many of the walls and ceilings, and much of the furniture was custom designed. The stair hall is highlighted by a dramatic domed ceiling, which is illuminated by a cupola and ornamented with a custom-designed staircase fashioned from a combination of gunmetal, bronze, and mahogany. The overall effect is one of lightness and delicacy with a nod to the Asian influence that inspired the design.

Opposite: *The entrance façade was designed to resemble a Regency style pavilion infused with French and Asian influences.*

Above: *The breakfast room and porch overlook Long Island Sound.*

A computer design rendering of the entrance façade (top) and garden façade (below).

Above: *The entrance façade highlights the rich interplay between the Kasota stone, clay tile roof, and the Indiana limestone accents.*

Following pages: *The rear of the house, viewed from its gardens.*

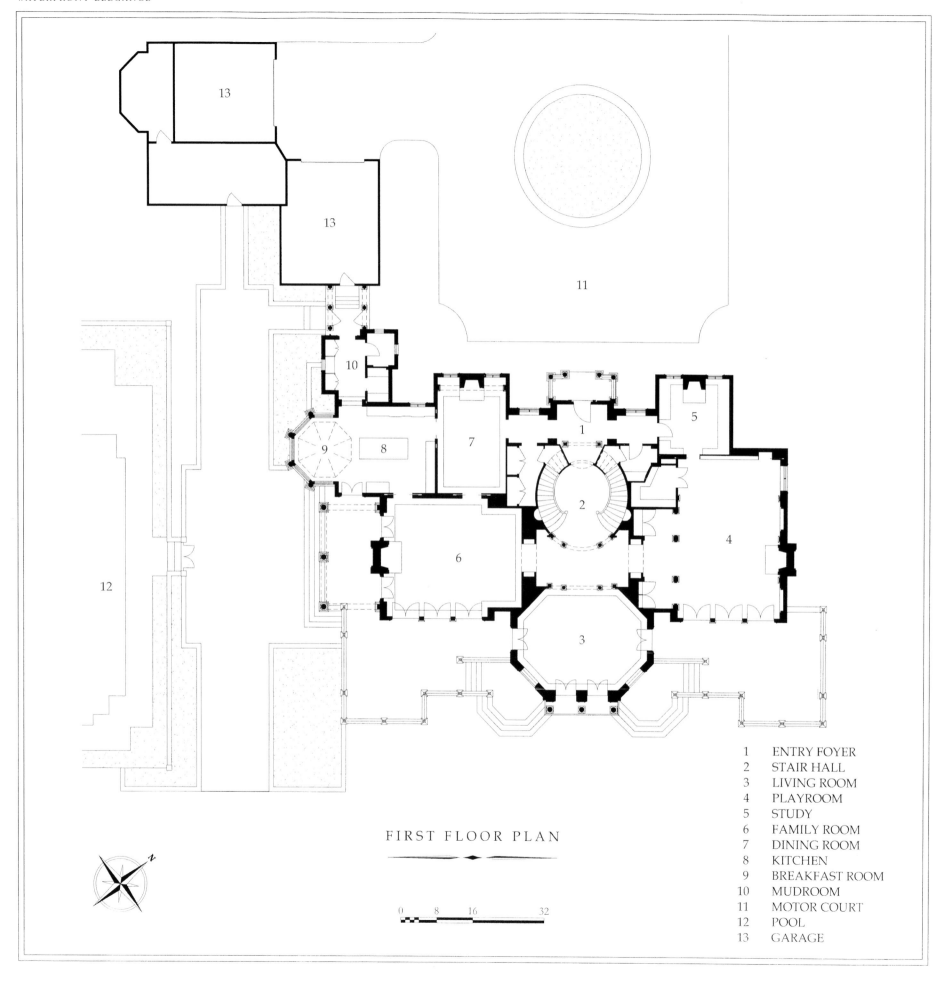

FIRST FLOOR PLAN

1   ENTRY FOYER
2   STAIR HALL
3   LIVING ROOM
4   PLAYROOM
5   STUDY
6   FAMILY ROOM
7   DINING ROOM
8   KITCHEN
9   BREAKFAST ROOM
10   MUDROOM
11   MOTOR COURT
12   POOL
13   GARAGE

0   8   16   32

A view from the kitchen, overlooking the breakfast porch and Long Island Sound beyond.

Details of the intricate plasterwork, chinoiserie-inspired millwork, and custom-designed staircase, which is fashioned from a combination of gunmetal, bronze, and mahogany.

The stair hall rotunda features faux-painted marble columns, a decoratively painted domed ceiling, and a custom-designed handrail.

The family room offers views of Long Island Sound.

The formal sitting room, decorated by Wadia, includes intricate moldings with gilded accents.

The media room is framed with custom-designed chinoiserie paneling.

The dining room is decorated with hand-painted Chinese wallpaper by Charles Gracie & Sons.

CLASSIC SHINGLE STYLE BEAUTY

New Canaan, Connecticut

WHAT IS IT ABOUT SHINGLE STYLE ARCHITECTURE that makes its imagery so seductive? This deliberately informal style—noteworthy for being so uniquely American—was first introduced as an architectural form in the 1880s by architects who were designing rustic summerhouses for their well-heeled clients in coastal New England communities. This classic beauty, which Wadia designed for a family in New Canaan, was inspired by the Isaac Bell House in Newport, Rhode Island. Widely considered to be the best remaining example of Shingle style architecture, the Isaac Bell House—designed by the prestigious firm of McKim, Mead, & White—is noteworthy for its colonial American detailing and a lack of fussiness that characterized earlier Queen Anne-influenced Shingle style homes.

Likewise, this Shingle style home is noteworthy for its simplified treatment of building trim and exterior surfaces. The front entry of the home features a vaulted porch, which leads into a double-height stair hall. Rising to the left of the porch is a tower reminiscent of a shingled lighthouse. On the first level, it houses an octagonal office from which the owners can keep an eye on who comes and goes through the front door. The second level houses their daughter's bedroom, a fanciful space reminiscent of Rapunzel's tower that fuels her imagination every time she gazes out the windows. To balance the heft and scale of the tower, Wadia clustered the gables of the house and sheathed several of them in wavy board shingles for artistic effect.

The floor plan of the house is organized around the generously proportioned stair hall, which is noteworthy for its highly unique staircase. In a nod to the Arts & Crafts movement, the custom-designed staircase features hand-turned balusters in an alternating corkscrew pattern and finely carved finials on the newel posts. An open floor plan, which eliminates corridors and doors, promotes the flow of air and light and transforms every nook into an informal gathering space. One particularly inviting space is the billiards room, which features floor-to-ceiling burled oak paneling. The exceptional craftsmanship and luxurious materials that make this room so inviting are also on display in the kitchen, which was custom designed by Wadia. A one-of-a-kind kitchen rangehood and false drawer fronts filled with colorful sweets are just two of the rich details that abound throughout the house. Ornamental yet highly functional, they provide the distinctive accents that give this home its much-loved character.

Opposite: *A design rendering of the front façade.*

Above: *The front façade features a series of asymmetrical elements such as the clustered gables, oriel window, and octagonal tower.*

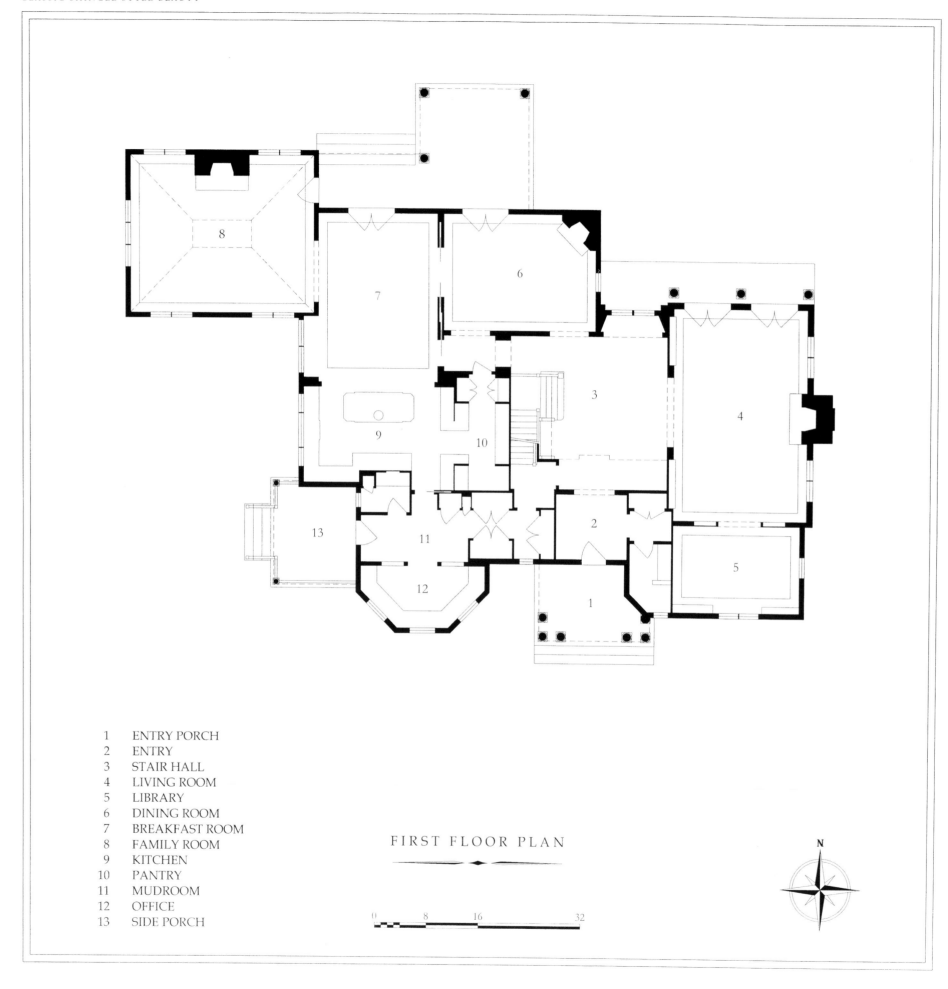

1   ENTRY PORCH
2   ENTRY
3   STAIR HALL
4   LIVING ROOM
5   LIBRARY
6   DINING ROOM
7   BREAKFAST ROOM
8   FAMILY ROOM
9   KITCHEN
10   PANTRY
11   MUDROOM
12   OFFICE
13   SIDE PORCH

FIRST FLOOR PLAN

0   8   16   32

N

The side entry highlights the use of simplified materials found in American Shingle design.

The floor plan of the house is organized around the stair hall and its Arts & Crafts-inspired staircase.

The hand-turned balusters are laid out in an alternating corkscrew pattern.

The living room features a custom-designed Arts & Crafts style fireplace.

A view from the living room into the billiard room.

A view from the living room overlooking the garden porch and terraces.

This oval spider-web window frames a view of the columns outside.

The pantry includes matching china and silver cabinets crafted from oak.

The family kitchen features custom-designed cabinets and a rangehood fabricated from brass and copper.

The open floor plan allows rooms to flow into each other.

The family room includes built-in cabinets, a cathedral ceiling, and a large fireplace.

FRENCH CHARM
IN BACK-COUNTRY GREENWICH

Greenwich, Connecticut

THE DESIGN OF THIS RESIDENCE, located in the Greenwich Back Country and overlooking the playing fields of the Greenwich Polo Club, was inspired while the owners were on vacation in the countryside of France. During their travels, they fell in love with the French Chateau style of architecture and its old-world charm. Upon their return, they scrapped their original plans for a Georgian style home and asked Wadia to design a French country manor instead. The stone construction, steeply pitched mansard roof, corner tower, hipped dormer windows, and wrought iron balconies are very much in keeping with the French tradition. Yet a separate wing housing the garage extending from the front right-hand corner of the house represents a deliberate departure from the symmetrical nature of the French Chateau style. To restore authenticity, Wadia created the illusion of symmetry with a large square motor court centered on the front entry hall of the house. The sense of symmetry is further enhanced by custom-designed wrought iron entrance gates, which were set on a direct axis to frame the view of the main body of the house.

The house is sited to accommodate, and complement, an existing apple orchard that was picturesquely laid out in a symmetrical manner. Following this example, Wadia constructed the surrounding landscape in the French style featuring formal gardens and highly structured geometric spaces—creating a synthesis and integration between the architecture and the property. The site plan for the property was also developed with the owners' love for horses and polo in mind—thus, all the living spaces of the home overlook the playing fields. A tall stone wall surrounding the motor court and swimming pool area creates a wonderful sense of enclosure and visually links these separate "outdoor rooms" to the house. A stone pavilion opens out to the pool on one side and provides a lovely view of the clipped, formal garden on the other side. Medieval in feel, the pavilion features the same steeply pitched roof as the house, ocular openings to capture the light, and well-defined stone arches all around. In a recurring architectural theme, the arches are repeated in the motor court arcade and the stone gazebos that provide passage from one garden space to the next. This creates a sense of overall continuity as one moves between the house and its gardens, and it becomes clear that the success of each is dependent on the other.

Opposite: *The formal gardens with the apple orchard and polo fields beyond.*

Above: *The front of the house is framed through the custom-designed wrought iron entrance gates.*

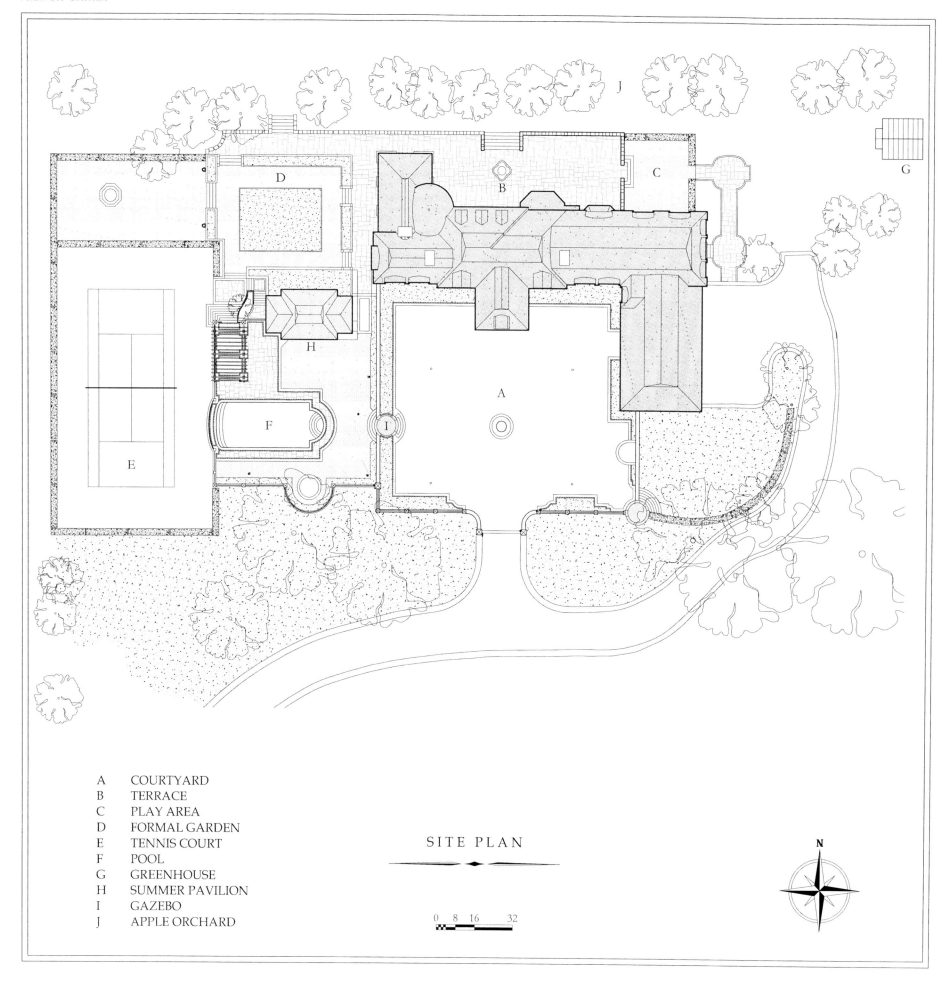

A   COURTYARD
B   TERRACE
C   PLAY AREA
D   FORMAL GARDEN
E   TENNIS COURT
F   POOL
G   GREENHOUSE
H   SUMMER PAVILION
I   GAZEBO
J   APPLE ORCHARD

SITE PLAN

0 8 16   32

N

The garden façade features a corner tower, mansard roof, iron balconies, and conservatory—all in keeping with the French tradition.

An arched stone arcade flanks the motor court.

The second-floor bay window, supported by brackets, overlooks the formal gardens.

One of the garden gazebos that provides passage from one garden space to the next.

The greenhouse and potting shed were added later, and designed to complement the architecture of the main house.

The open loggia of the summer pavilion.

The summer pavilion opens to the swimming pool on one side, and overlooks the formal gardens on the other.

Details of how architectural elements have been added to the landscape design to further enrich the dialogue between the house and its gardens.

The tennis court is nestled into the gardens, and is surrounded by hornbeam hedges to conceal the metal fencing.

The stone gazebo, framing a view of the motor court, features exposed oak roof trusses.

The custom-designed wrought iron entrance gate.

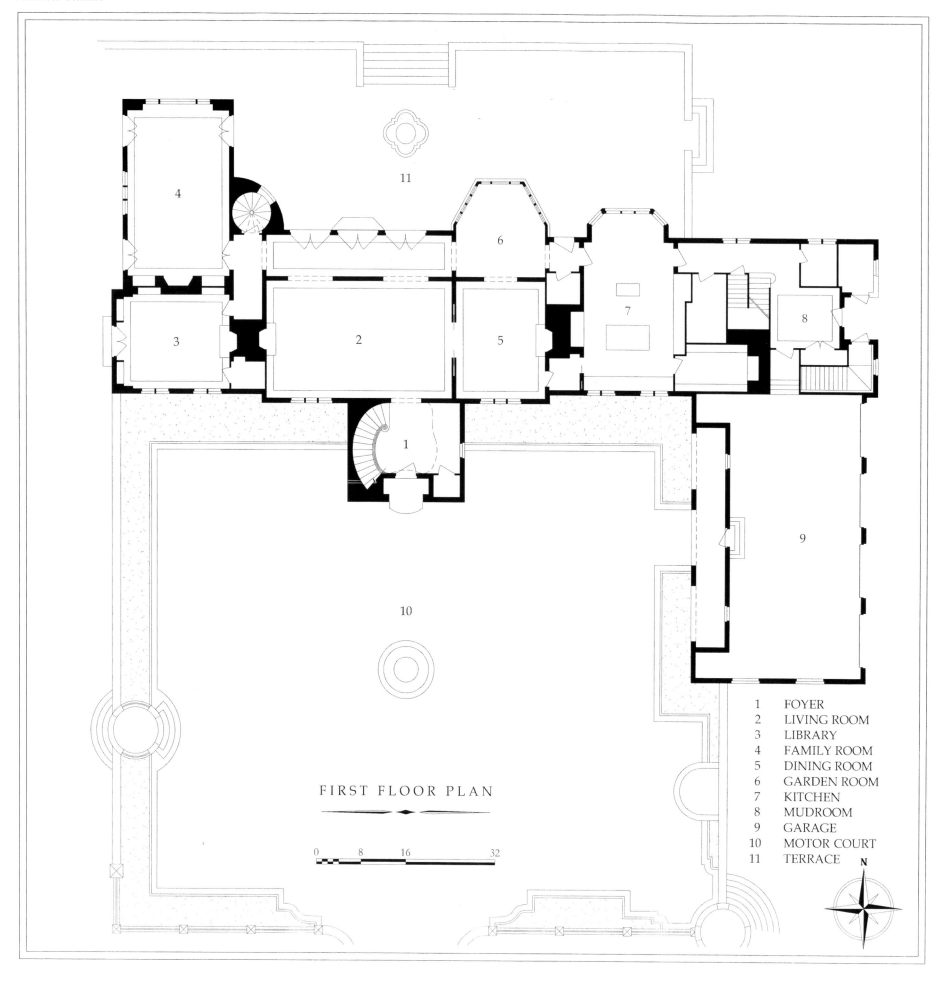

FIRST FLOOR PLAN

0   8   16   32

1   FOYER
2   LIVING ROOM
3   LIBRARY
4   FAMILY ROOM
5   DINING ROOM
6   GARDEN ROOM
7   KITCHEN
8   MUDROOM
9   GARAGE
10   MOTOR COURT
11   TERRACE

N

The spiral staircase is custom designed with iron and bronze details.

The dining room is separated from the conservatory by decorative lattice-work, which allows views of the garden beyond.

The gallery, featuring an arched lattice ceiling, links all the principal rooms and overlooks the garden terrace.

The kitchen, designed in the French Provincial style, includes exposed wood beams and a brick oven.

The cavernous wine cellar and tasting room includes stone arches, and features custom-designed wrought iron details throughout.

The private sitting room in the master suite.

The children's playroom is located above the garage.

A GEORGIAN CLASSIC
WITH A MODERN TWIST

New Canaan, Connecticut

THE DESIGN OF THIS COUNTRY HOUSE was inspired by the work of Virginia architect, William Lawrence Bottomley (1883–1951), whose neo-Georgian houses are generally considered the finest examples of domestic Georgian architecture built in the 1920s and 1930s. Evocative of his style, the house is deliberately conservative yet rife with sophisticated and beautiful details that infuse it with a certain playfulness. The heavily detailed entrance portico features Ionic columns, finely carved dentils, and leaded glass windows in the sidelights and transom. Brick quoins and recessed panels provide crisp definition to the exterior of the house, while the proportions of the first- and second-floor windows lend a wonderful sense of hierarchy to the overall structure. With delicate wrought iron balconies and solid shutters, the first-floor windows are both taller and grander than the second-floor windows, a characteristic feature of Georgian architecture meant to reflect the importance of the rooms behind.

While classic Georgian style evolved during the nearly 120 years that comprised the Georgian period (from the accession of George I in 1714 to the death of George IV in 1830), it always remained faithful to one defining element: the grand symmetrical façade. Life in the 21st century, however, defies symmetry. Families today place a premium on comfort and convenience. They want functional spaces never envisioned during the Georgian period—a family room, mud room, breakfast room, and multi-car garage—and they want these spaces clustered close to the kitchen, which has grown in size and prominence to become the heart of the home. Together with the dining room, this cluster of functional spaces leads to a lopsided floor plan, a contradiction of the very essence of Georgian architecture. To resolve this dilemma and preserve the home's symmetry, Wadia placed the garage, mudroom, and family room in a separate wing, which was set back considerably from the main body of the residence and partially tucked behind the rear elevation. This imaginative reinterpretation of traditional design renders the house both modern and livable while remaining faithful to classic Georgian style.

Opposite: *A design rendering of the front façade.*

Above: *The façade includes many subtle details such as differing window sizes and shutter designs, as well as recessed brick panels.*

Details of the playful architectural elements added to the façade include scrolled brackets at the dormer windows, a cartouche window surround in the pediment, Ionic capitals at the entrance porch, and stone finials.

The entrance porch is delicately detailed in the Ionic order.

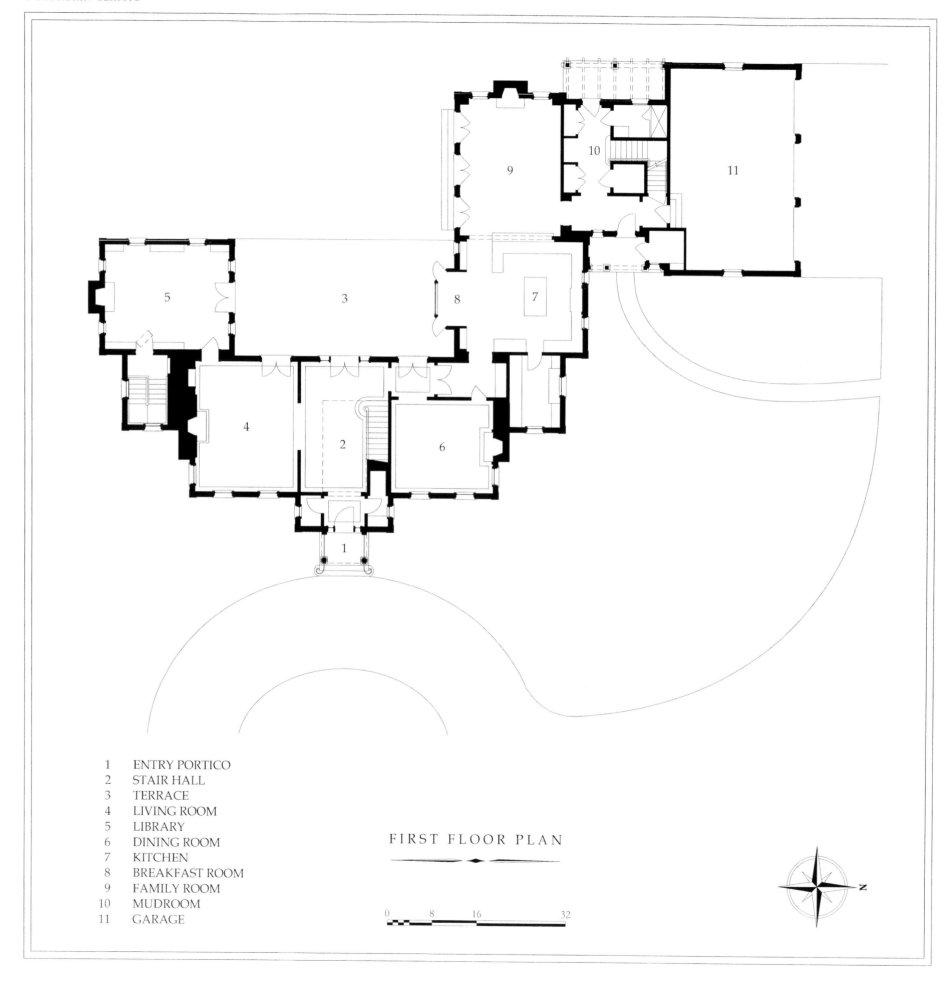

1   ENTRY PORTICO
2   STAIR HALL
3   TERRACE
4   LIVING ROOM
5   LIBRARY
6   DINING ROOM
7   KITCHEN
8   BREAKFAST ROOM
9   FAMILY ROOM
10 MUDROOM
11 GARAGE

FIRST FLOOR PLAN

0   8   16   32

N

The family room, viewed from the kitchen, opens out to the garden terrace.

VICTORIAN REFINEMENT
INFUSED WITH ARTS & CRAFTS CHARM

Greenwich, Connecticut

KNOWN AS ROSEMARY HALL, this beautiful stucco and stone home was designed by Henry C. Pelton in 1902 as the residence for the principal of Rosemary Hall School. With its fairy-tale charm, it is reasonable to assume that the house fueled the imagination of more than a few students who graced the campus of this all-girls' school. Featuring fanciful wood trim, distinctive brick chimneys, and pointed finials perched atop the steeply peaked roof, one half expects Hansel and Gretel to stumble out of the woods onto the cobbled motor court.

Despite its obvious visual appeal, however, over time the house had become antiquated and was in desperate need of updating to adequately serve the needs and modern lifestyle of its current owners. The solution required a substantial addition to the home to create multifunctional spaces for casual day-to-day living. Seamlessly woven into the charm of the original home is a spacious new family room with three-quarter height wainscoting and beamed ceilings, stylistic features often found in houses inspired by the Arts & Crafts movement, and a fireplace fashioned with antique de Morgan Isnik tiled panels. Adjoining this space is the kitchen, which, with its coffered ceiling, decorative brackets, floor-to-ceiling paneling, and finely hand-crafted cabinetry, displays a reverence for craftsmanship rarely found today. Leading from the kitchen is a new informal dining area, a favorite gathering spot for the family, which overlooks the lush garden through a broad bay window. As part of the addition, Wadia added a new office and guest suite as well as a new side porch with curved brackets, barge boards, and newels that echo the details of the original home. Taken together, these new spaces have become the heart of the home—inviting and livable with all the modern amenities that today's homeowners have come to expect. Yet, the classic style and details of the original home remain intact, reminding one and all of the history of this fine old home.

Opposite: *A computer design rendering of the street façade.*

Above: *The new entrance to the house as seen from the motor court.*

Detail of a new dormer window.

The new garden façade features decorative half timbering in keeping with that on the existing house.

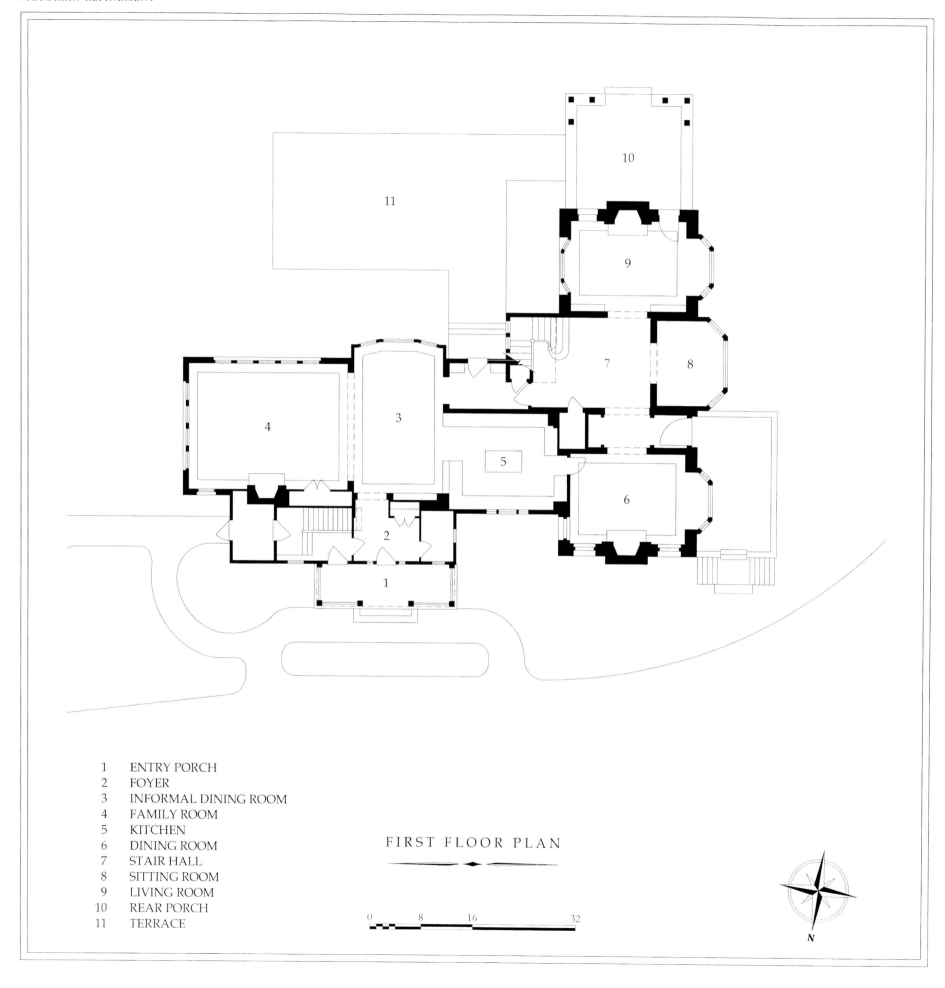

FIRST FLOOR PLAN

1　ENTRY PORCH
2　FOYER
3　INFORMAL DINING ROOM
4　FAMILY ROOM
5　KITCHEN
6　DINING ROOM
7　STAIR HALL
8　SITTING ROOM
9　LIVING ROOM
10　REAR PORCH
11　TERRACE

0　　8　　16　　32

The family room, features three-quarter-height wainscoting, a fireplace fashioned with antique de Morgan Isnik tiles, and a cathedral ceiling.

The intimate breakfast room overlooks the terrace and gardens.

The kitchen, crafted in oak, features floor-to-ceiling cabinetry and paneling.

A TASTE OF TUSCANY

Greenwich, Connecticut

Dubbed "the castle" by locals, this turn-of-the-century home situated at the top of a hill gained its moniker from its resemblance to one of the many fortified Tuscan castles that dot the hilltops of Italy. The home's medieval feel is enhanced by a stone gatehouse and an imposing campanile, or bell tower, which rises above a porte-cochère and lends a distinctly feudal presence to the residence.

Despite the sense of permanence its structure suggests, the house was in great need of repair by the time the current owners retained Wadia to undertake its restoration. As part of the renovation, they also wanted to update the home to include more modern amenities such as a larger, more luxurious master bedroom and an outdoor spa.

In a thoughtful balance between respect for traditional architecture and the contemporary needs of his clients, Wadia increased the footprint of the home to include an addition for a new master bedroom suite. Included in the expanded space is a generously sized bathroom with his-and-hers vanities, separate showers and his-and-hers dressing closets. He also added a terrace off the back of the house featuring a sunken garden and outdoor spa for the family. In what ultimately became a feat of engineering, Wadia dropped the foundation of the home by several feet to create a proper walkout basement to access the spa from what was originally little more than a crawl space under the home.

As part of the restoration, all of the stonework on the façade of the house was re-pointed, the house was re-roofed, and the interior of the home was completely gutted and renovated. From the existing interior space, Wadia created a new study with rich, dark mahogany paneling. It achieves a bright and airy feel from its coffered ceiling, which features delicate rosettes and gilded moldings. Likewise, the same exceptional workmanship is on display in the informal dining room. Antique doors fitted with lovely leaded glass panes perpetuate the medieval feel of the home, one of thousands of design details that distinguishes all of Wadia's work.

Opposite: *The fully restored house and addition as seen from the motor court.*

Above: *The addition (on the left) blends in seamlessly with the existing house.*

Design renderings showing the addition as seen from the driveway (above) and the motor court (below).

The new outdoor terrace and spa area.

The fireplace in the living room was restored, and a new decorative paneled ceiling was added to complement the design.

A view into the remodeled breakfast room, with new three-quarter-height wainscoting and decorative paneled ceiling.

The study features new mahogany paneled walls, and a custom-designed coffered ceiling resplendent with rosettes and gilded mouldings.

The master bedroom includes an antique marble fireplace and paneled walls.

ADIRONDACK STYLE HOMESTEAD

New Canaan, Connecticut

LOCATED ON 16 WOODED ACRES on an old Indian reservation, this Adirondack style home built by Wadia in the mid-1990s offers plenty of seclusion amid the natural beauty of its setting. The use of indigenous natural materials for the façade of the house serves to tie it to the surrounding landscape. Wood shingling and timber detailing features whimsical flourishes, such as the fir trees carved into the shutters.

Mindful of the owners' request for an informal, family-friendly home, Wadia designed the home with an open floor plan that promotes the flow of air and light. Broad, welcoming openings join the various spaces rather than corridors to accommodate the comings and goings of this busy, modern family. Throughout the interior of the house, finely crafted decorative features set off the family's arts and crafts collection. Sausage columns in the bedroom delineate a separate niche for the sitting area, which has been richly decorated with folk art. Similarly, numerous woodworking details in the bathroom, including dropped finials over the bathtub and beaded board wainscoting, combine to create a homey, casual feel. The overall result is as warm and inviting as it is sophisticated—creating a truly wonderful retreat for the family to gather.

Opposite: *The entrance porch.*

Above: *The house is nestled into the landscape.*

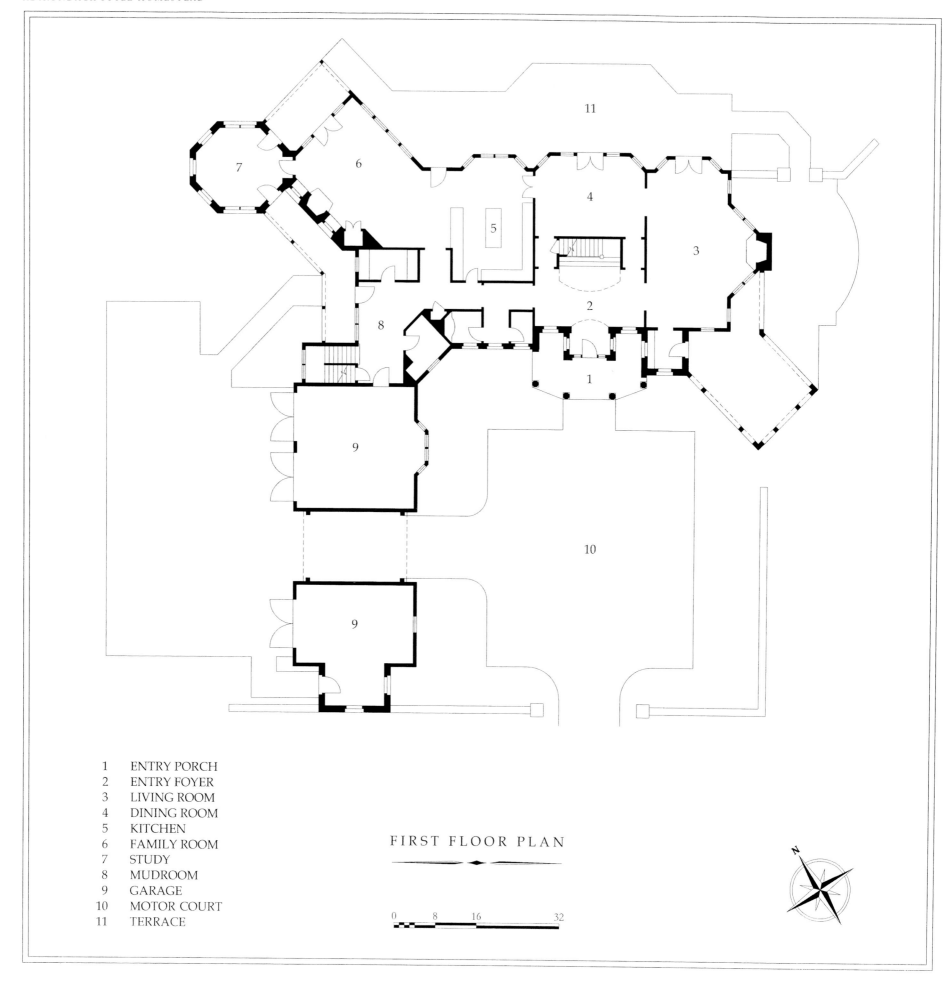

FIRST FLOOR PLAN

1   ENTRY PORCH
2   ENTRY FOYER
3   LIVING ROOM
4   DINING ROOM
5   KITCHEN
6   FAMILY ROOM
7   STUDY
8   MUDROOM
9   GARAGE
10   MOTOR COURT
11   TERRACE

0   8   16   32

Flowing from the kitchen, the relaxed and playful family room is richly decorated with folk art.

The sitting room niche is separated from the master bedroom by the Arts & Crafts-inspired sausage columns.

The bathroom features dropped finials over the tub, and beaded board on the walls.

BACK-COUNTRY ELEGANCE
WITH DOWNTOWN CONVENIENCE

Greenwich, Connecticut

WITH ITS WINDING COUNTRY LANES, rambling stone walls, and magnificent estates, the heavily wooded "back-country" in the northern section of Greenwich has a well-deserved reputation for being one of America's most prestigious addresses. While its considerable distance from downtown Greenwich is an obvious advantage for those who cherish a quiet existence, it can be a bit too remote for active families who regularly frequent the town's shops, businesses, and schools. For homeowners who long for both a wonderful country estate and easy access to town, Wadia has designed two distinctive homes with classic style located within a short walking distance to downtown Greenwich.

The first residence is a Greek Revival style home that was designed to seem like a centuries-old formal house that had been added onto over the years. The second residence is a classically styled Georgian home featuring the formal symmetry typical of this type of architecture. Although each house is set on just half an acre, the homes are spacious nonetheless and nicely complement the many impressive homes in the surrounding area. Although the overall footprint of each of the two homes is necessarily smaller than the average Wadia-designed home given the acreage of the lots, the same amount of function is designed into the smaller space. By incorporating an open floor plan that reduces the amount of circulation space between rooms—hallways are eliminated in favor of rooms that flow into one another—Wadia was able to offer interior rooms that are classically proportioned and offer roughly the same square footage as his larger-scale residences. Each of the homes includes four bedrooms with bathrooms, a wine cellar, two staircases, fireplaces in all the major rooms, a spacious pantry, outdoor porches, and a paneled study. Featuring both substance and style, these homes offer back-country elegance with downtown convenience—the perfect union for today's active family.

Opposite: *The front façade of the Georgian style home viewed from the street.*

Above: *Although differing in styles, both houses fit into the eclectic fabric of Fairfield County.*

Design renderings of the Greek Revival home (above) and the Georgian home (below).

The side entrance porch of the Greek Revival style home.

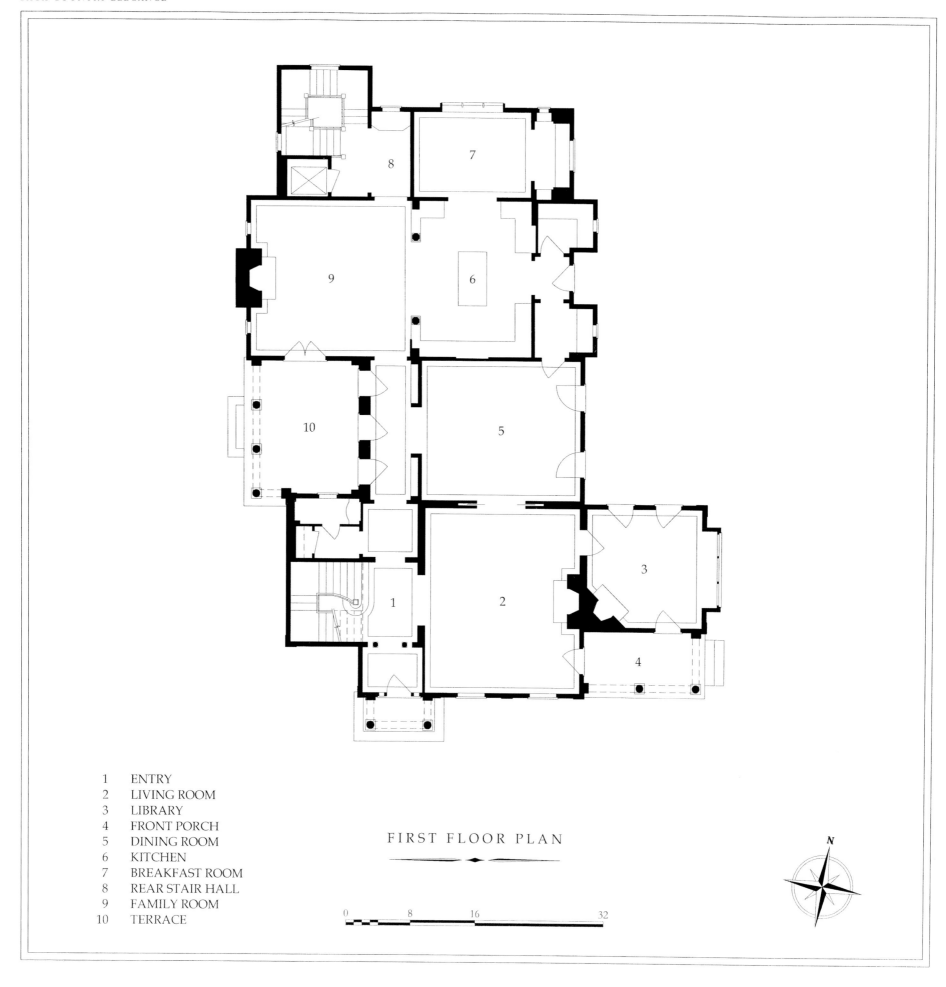

1   ENTRY
2   LIVING ROOM
3   LIBRARY
4   FRONT PORCH
5   DINING ROOM
6   KITCHEN
7   BREAKFAST ROOM
8   REAR STAIR HALL
9   FAMILY ROOM
10 TERRACE

FIRST FLOOR PLAN

0   8   16   32

N

The Greek Revival style home is designed and massed asymmetrically to resemble a structure that has been added onto over the years.

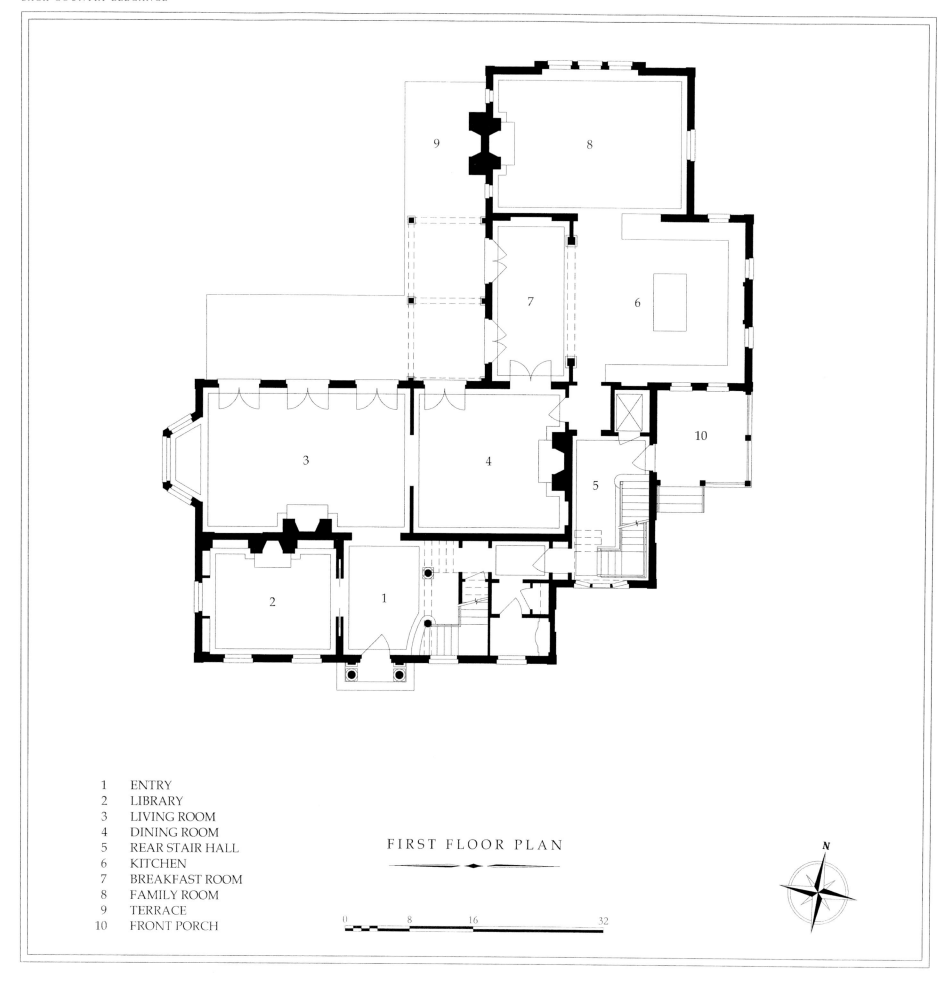

FIRST FLOOR PLAN

1   ENTRY
2   LIBRARY
3   LIVING ROOM
4   DINING ROOM
5   REAR STAIR HALL
6   KITCHEN
7   BREAKFAST ROOM
8   FAMILY ROOM
9   TERRACE
10 FRONT PORCH

0   8   16   32

N

The formal front of the Georgian style home is symmetrical in nature, and has the family wing tucked behind it.

QUINTESSENTIALLY ENGLISH
A COUNTRY HOUSE AND GARDENS

North Salem, New York

THE ROLLING HILLS NORTH OF NEW YORK CITY, which feature some of the most dramatic scenery in the region, have been horse country for the past three centuries. The landscape features sweeping views of wooded hillsides while barns, pastures, and horse paddocks provide vernacular reminders of its agrarian past. Taking his cue from this magnificent setting, Wadia sought to create a dialogue between the design of the home and the surrounding landscape. To emphasize the views of an adjacent nature conservancy, he sited the home carefully and designed a floor plan that would capture the outdoor beauty at every turn. He also manipulated the transitional spaces around the exterior of the house with a series of well-defined garden rooms to force a particular view or perspective. By emphasizing these transitions—visitors must walk through a small entry garden that overlooks a larger formal garden before they can turn right to get to the front door, for example—guests experience a sense of discovery as they move through the landscape.

The owners of the home, who are both avid gardeners, wanted to be able to wake up in the morning and walk directly into the garden. Accordingly, the master bedroom is situated on the first floor, as are all of the other essential rooms, while the guest bedrooms occupy the second floor. Tender plants are over-wintered in the conservatory, a warm and inviting room with a double-height ceiling, exposed timbering and trusses, and lovely double-height bay windows that flood the room with sunlight. The central corridor is designed with arched casings framing the doorways, which open up the space and extend the view to the garden beyond. The living room, which features a limestone fireplace mantle and floor-to-ceiling wood paneling, has been deliberately designed with large windows to capture the dramatic view of the nature conservancy. Naturally, this is a tricky proposition as oversized windows are not in the language of traditional classical design. Yet, with a bit of inventiveness, the windows have been classically re-imagined and deftly incorporated into the traditional styling of the home. In fact, the home itself, and the way it is intimately linked to the landscape by its gardens and vistas, looks as though it could have been plucked from the English countryside.

Opposite: *A design rendering showing a panoramic view of the garden façade.*

Above: *A view of the garden façade overlooking the swimming pool.*

Design renderings showing the entrance forecourt with its formal garden and oriel window (above), and the front entry flanked by the bay window of the conservatory (below).

Although asymmetrical in design, the differing architectural elements of the design create a welcoming entrance courtyard.

The entrance to the home is quintessentially restrained—in keeping with the rustic nature of the English country Arts & Crafts style.

The conservatory is dominated by the pair of double-height bay windows, and the exposed wood roof trusses.

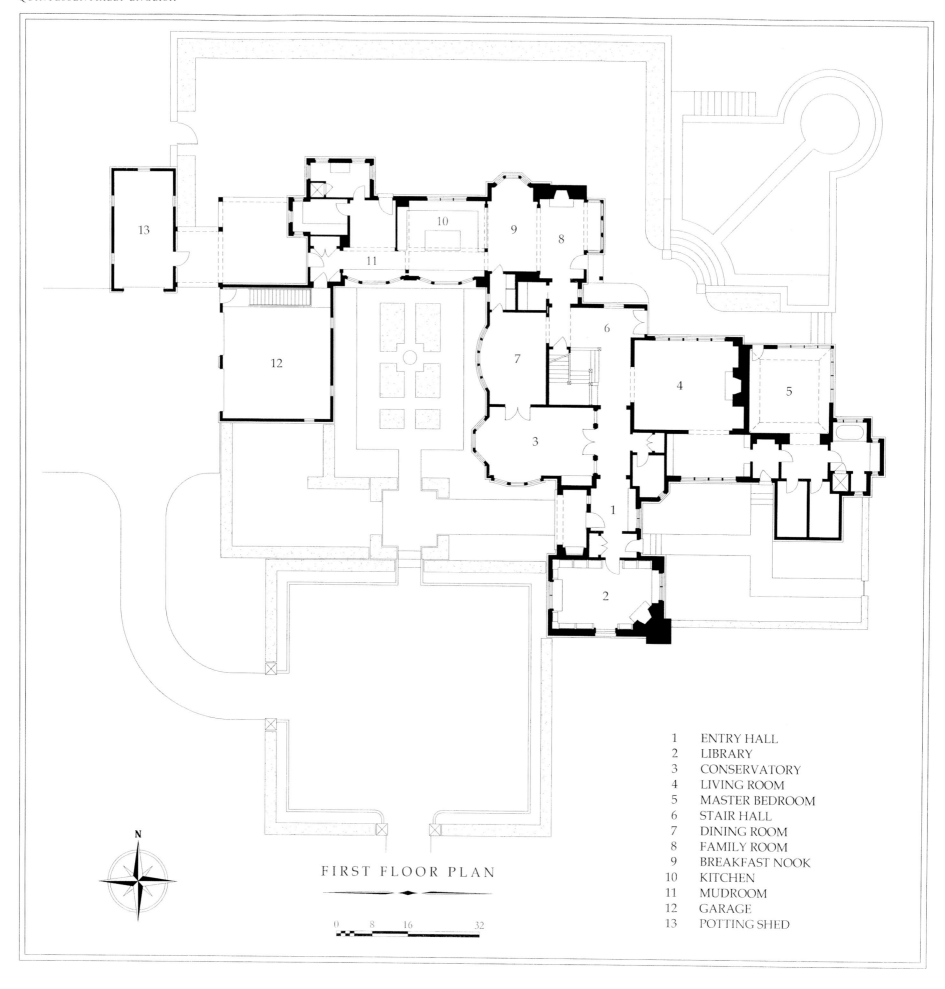

FIRST FLOOR PLAN

0   8   16   32

1   ENTRY HALL
2   LIBRARY
3   CONSERVATORY
4   LIVING ROOM
5   MASTER BEDROOM
6   STAIR HALL
7   DINING ROOM
8   FAMILY ROOM
9   BREAKFAST NOOK
10 KITCHEN
11 MUDROOM
12 GARAGE
13 POTTING SHED

The oak-paneled living room has all the charm found in an authentic English manor house.

Details of the custom-designed limestone fireplaces and the hand-carved millwork that are found throughout the house.

The stair hall features an Arts & Crafts style staircase with built-in bench, hand crafted in oak.

Arched openings in the entrance hall frame the axial view to the library.

The master bedroom, with its tray ceiling, opens directly out to the manicured formal gardens.

AN ENGLISH POTTING SHED

New Canaan, Connecticut

BUILT INTO A HILLSIDE on the grounds of a country cottage in New Canaan, this lovely potting shed is as functional as it is aesthetically pleasing. In addition to a potting room, the stone structure has two large greenhouses—a hothouse for over-wintering tropical plants and a warmhouse for propagating annuals and perennials—both of which overlook a generously proportioned courtyard. The potting shed is accessed through an enclosed sunken entry garden that leads to an open-air loggia. A stone staircase featuring a finely crafted wrought iron balustrade offers a dramatic ascent from the loggia to a second-story apartment. Occupying the entire second floor, the apartment serves as the living quarters for the estate's resident horticulturist, who oversees the maintenance of the property's extensive gardens. The first story of the potting shed is constructed from Minnesota Kasota stone with carved limestone surrounds framing the doors and windows. The walls of the upper story are sheathed in the same English clay tiles that have been used for the steeply pitched roof. This mixture of exterior surface materials, combined with the use of oak wooden beams and posts for the interior, and rustic paneled doors throughout—so highly reminiscent of the English Arts & Crafts style—are but a few of the extraordinary details that infuse the potting shed with its distinctive flair.

Opposite: *A design rendering of the garden façade.*

Above: *The potting shed was constructed using Minnesota Kasota stone, Indiana limestone, reclaimed oak, and English clay tiles.*

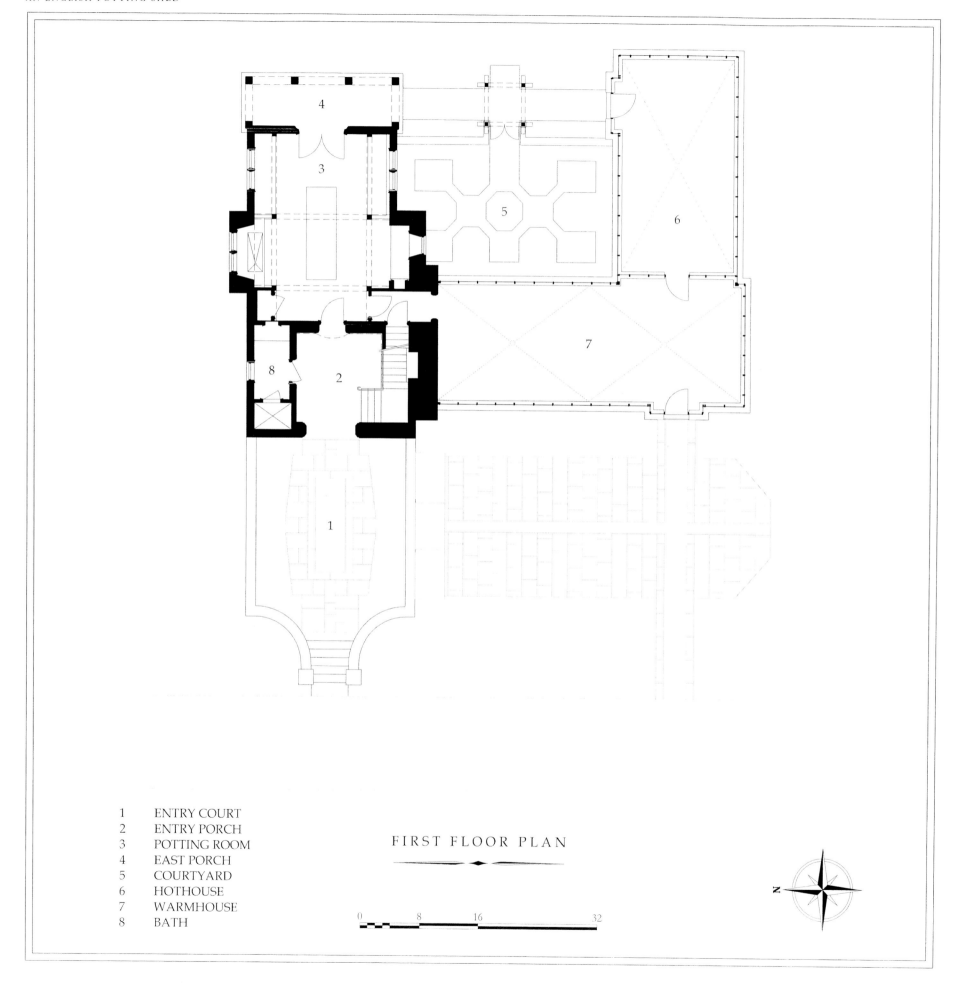

1   ENTRY COURT
2   ENTRY PORCH
3   POTTING ROOM
4   EAST PORCH
5   COURTYARD
6   HOTHOUSE
7   WARMHOUSE
8   BATH

FIRST FLOOR PLAN

0   8   16   32

The potting shed is accessed through an enclosed sunken garden that leads directly into the open loggia.

The Arts & Crafts style potting room features oak posts and beams, as well as custom-designed oak doors.

Open to the elements, the loggia includes a staircase that leads to a second-floor apartment.

GATSBY-ESQUE GRANDEUR
ON BLOCK ISLAND SOUND

Watch Hill, Rhode Island

IT ISN'T HARD TO IMAGINE JAY GATSBY gazing out across the glittering waters of Block Island Sound from the terrace of this magnificent Tudor home designed by the renowned architect, John Russell Pope (1874–1937). Best known for his designs of public buildings, churches, museums, and monuments, including the American Museum of Natural History in New York, The National Gallery, and Jefferson Memorial in Washington, D.C., Pope was nonetheless a consummate designer of country houses, most of which were completed during the early part of his career. Given his respect for Pope, whose architectural achievements greatly inspired him and had a profound impact on his eventual design philosophy, Wadia felt a great sense of obligation when he undertook the renovation and subsequent additions to this outstanding home. Recognizing the foolishness of attempting to improve upon a master, it became Wadia's unspoken responsibility to ensure that the style and dignity of the home remained unaltered, an exercise in ego suppression lest he inadvertently place a stamp where none was needed.

The renovation of the house began with the façade, which had deteriorated significantly over time. Wadia revitalized the rear terrace, an impressive structure running along the entire length of the house. By replacing the timber posts with stone piers and incorporating a new rear portico into its overall design, the terrace is now better fortified to withstand the salt sprays and has become a wonderful gathering spot to relax and enjoy the magnificent views. As the renovation proceeded, it became apparent that several additions would be necessary to update the home. The first addition off one side of the house created space for an enlarged kitchen and breakfast room on the first level, topped by a graciously appointed master suite featuring a dressing room, sitting room, and his-and-hers bathrooms on the second level. On the opposite side of the house, a second addition was designed to provide space for a new family room overlooking the swimming pool. A third addition features a new garage wing that connects the main house to the guest house. The additions are incorporated into the overall design of the house so seamlessly that more than one observer has been prompted to marvel at its authenticity. Of course, to have his design modifications mistaken for Pope's work is the greatest compliment that Wadia could ever receive.

Opposite: *A design rendering showing the restored house with its additions.*

Above: *The addition seamlessly blends in with the architecture of the existing house.*

Previous pages: *A panoramic view of the fully restored waterfront façade and gardens.*

Above: *A view of the house before the renovation work began.*

Below: *The same view after construction showing the fully restored house and gardens, as well as the additions.*

The new family room (on the right) opens out onto a new terrace and swimming pool.

The fully restored covered terrace runs the entire length of the house and offers spectacular waterfront views.

The double-height music room, with its half timbering and mezzanine, was fully restored by Wadia.

STATELY AMERICAN COLONIAL

New Canaan, Connecticut

THE PROVENANCE OF THIS PICTURESQUE COLONIAL, built in 1905, is almost as intriguing as the home itself. It is rumored to have been designed by the legendary architect, Stanford White (1853–1906), of the renowned firm of McKim, Mead & White. Heralded as the most prominent architect of The Gilded Age, White's sensational murder by the husband of a former mistress tragically cut short a glittering career. While no architectural plans for the house exist, the extraordinary quality of the home is consistent with White's work. Originally built in typically American Colonial fashion, the residence exhibited the rectangular symmetry associated with this style. Over the years, however, it had been added on to, resulting in an asymmetrical composition that caused the front door to lose its prominence. This loss of stature created confusion for guests as they mistook a side door for the front entrance.

As part of an extensive renovation to update and remodel the residence, Wadia restored the hierarchy of the front door by replacing the entrance porch with a larger portico. Its wider opening provides greater functionality while many graceful flourishes, including the double Doric columns, carved dentils, and leaded glass windows in the sidelights and transom, give it a much grander presence. Wadia also replaced an existing window on the front façade with a highly decorative Palladian window. Composed of an arched central window flanked by two smaller symmetrical windows and framed by an Ionic entablature, the shape and ornamentation of the Palladian window lends charm to the house while softening its otherwise severe lines. New arched dormers, which echo the rounded shape of the window, offer additional visual appeal, as does the overhead balcony above the new rear porch. In true American fashion, the renovation of this gracious home—which also involved gutting and remodeling the interior of the house, replacing all the windows, re-shingling the roof, incorporating all new stonework, and adding a small addition—represents an inevitable progression of Colonial style. Its timeless beauty is a tribute to the evolutionary process inherent in architectural design in which the past must be reinterpreted to keep pace with the present.

Opposite: *The fully restored garden façade and new porch.*

Above: *The new entrance porch and Palladian window.*

The existing semi-circular open porch was converted into a new paneled library.

The front façade viewed from the driveway.

MEAD POINT TUDOR

Greenwich, Connecticut

THIS TUDOR ESTATE, modeled after Compton Wynyates in Warwickshire, England, is one of the last remaining Greenwich mansions built during the "Great Estate" era from 1880 to 1930. Built by Greenwich architect Edgar Self, the home boasts one of the loveliest natural settings on the Greenwich shorefront. The design of the home is distinctive for the half-timbering in the gables, the sharply pitched roofs with clustered chimneys, and the use of banks of windows of different sizes to give a feeling of openness.

Sadly, over the years the house had been badly neglected. In an extensive renovation begun in the early 1980s, Wadia completely restored the exterior of the house and made significant changes to the interior floor plan to reorganize the master suite. To repair the roof, all the slate tiles were removed and then replaced once repairs were completed. The red-hued bricks, which were specially made to imitate the small size and colors of those of Compton Wynyates, had to be cleaned and re-pointed. Likewise, all of the limestone accents around the windows were cleaned and re-pointed, and the lovely stained glass windows were cleaned and re-leaded. Much of the half-timbering had rotted and was replaced with matching wood, and all of the terraces were rebuilt. In addition, Wadia gutted and renovated the pool house and built a guest cottage on the property.

Today, fully restored to its former glory, the house stands as a reminder of a bygone era, where the giants of American trade and finance built summer "cottages" and ultimately created a unique architectural legacy.

Opposite: *The fully restored garden façade.*

Above: *The façade was extensively cleaned and repaired, and much of the half timbering was replaced.*

Details of the restored millwork, plasterwork, ironwork, and stained glass.

The stair hall was restored to its former glory.

PICTURESQUE QUEEN ANNE MANOR

Greenwich, Connecticut

ALTHOUGH ASYMMETRY IS A HALLMARK OF QUEEN ANNE ARCHITECTURE, the layout for this lovely waterfront residence was principally determined more by the funnel-shaped contours of the property. In addition, the owners asked that the house be as low key as possible—especially when viewed from the street and upon its approach. Accordingly, Wadia designed the home to unfold slowly with interesting twists and turns so that its overall size could never be taken in at once. All of the principal rooms were designed to overlook Long Island Sound, although in the warmer months the view is more often appreciated by the family from the wide porch that extends along the rear of the house.

In classic Queen Anne style, the house features a steeply pitched slate roof with highly decorative peak ornaments punctuating the fragmented roofline. Patterned shingles, overhanging stories, and an entrance tower combine to create the picturesque appeal so valued by this form of architecture. The detailing is also typically eclectic with medieval paneled chimneys, classical porch columns, and the use of a variety of exterior sheathing materials—fieldstone, brick, slate, and shingles. The result is a home that achieves a sense of romance and refinement in the best Queen Anne tradition.

Opposite: *A design rendering of the front of the house, as seen from the driveway.*

Above: *The house under construction, as viewed from the driveway.*

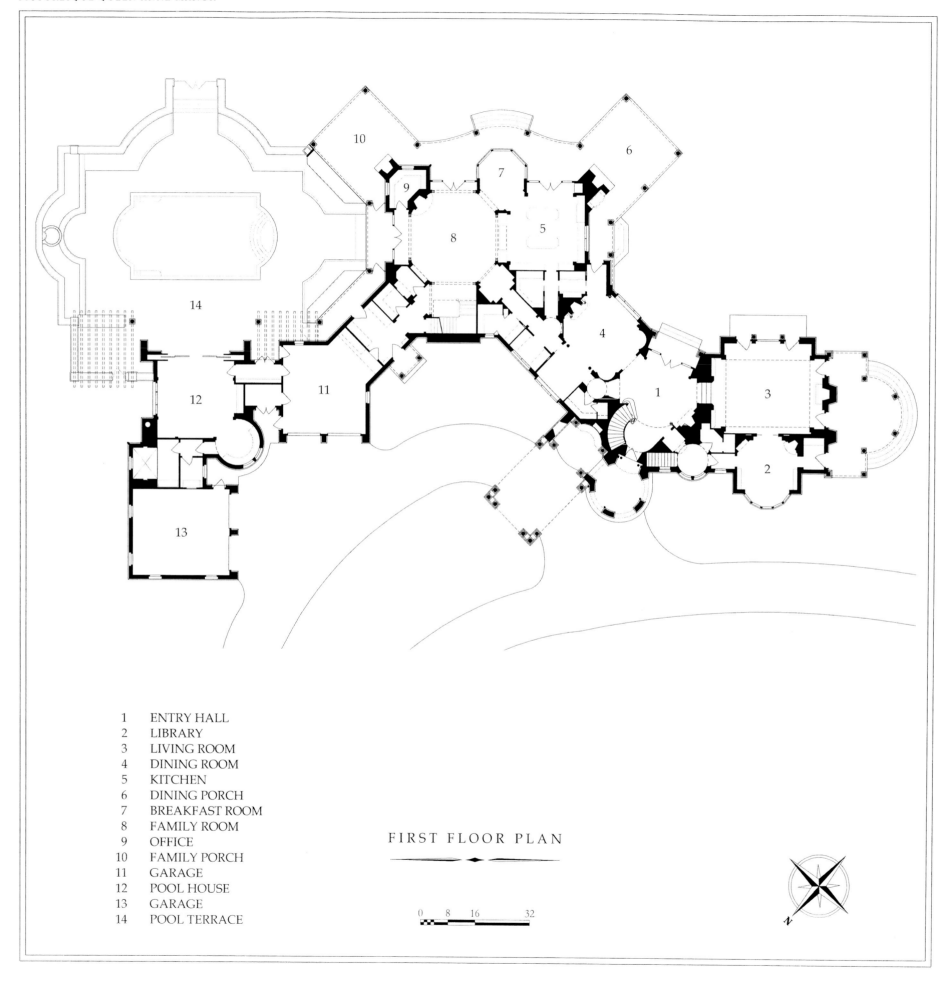

FIRST FLOOR PLAN

1   ENTRY HALL
2   LIBRARY
3   LIVING ROOM
4   DINING ROOM
5   KITCHEN
6   DINING PORCH
7   BREAKFAST ROOM
8   FAMILY ROOM
9   OFFICE
10 FAMILY PORCH
11 GARAGE
12 POOL HOUSE
13 GARAGE
14 POOL TERRACE

0   8   16   32

Details of the decorative Queen Anne motifs found on the house: fretwork at the gables, balconies, ornate fenestration, and decorative shingles.

ROMANTIC SHINGLE STYLE
WITH QUEEN ANNE MOTIFS

Weston, Connecticut

Above: *A design rendering of the front façade.*

Below: *The house under construction.*

ENGLISH ARTS & CRAFTS
MEETS AMERICAN SHINGLE STYLE

New Canaan, Connecticut

Above: *A design rendering of the front façade.*

Below: *The house under construction.*

PATTERN BOOK

A Question of Style

By
Francis Morrone

CONNECTICUT'S RESIDENTIAL ARCHITECTURE IS AS DIVERSE as any place in America, with examples ranging from earliest colonial times to the present day. Yet for all the differences in Connecticut architecture, for all its eclectic nature, there is also remarkable continuity. We see right away that grand country houses of the turn of the 20th century were influenced by the vernacular styles of colonial architecture of the 18th century.

The 18th-century architecture of Connecticut is often said to be the simple and handsome expression of old, self-effacing New England customs—as best seen in the Captain David Judson house (c. 1750) in Stratford. This and countless other houses in Connecticut have clapboarded fronts, pitched roofs with side gables, and six-over-six windows, typically with two to either side of the front door and two to either side of a window placed directly above the front door. The basic form was sometimes elaborated upon with the introduction of porches, pediments, or fanlights. A fine example of this is the Hanford-Silliman house (c. 1764) in New Canaan.

The 19th century brought a taste for the picturesque. The Lockwood-Mathews house (c. 1868), designed by Detlef Lienau, in Norwalk, and Edward Tuckerman Potter's house for Mark Twain (c. 1873), in the state capital of Hartford, are outstanding examples of Victorian picturesque eclecticism. By century's end, however, venerated architects such as McKim, Mead & White of New York City were designing Shingle style houses, like the John Howard Whittemore house (c. 1894–96) in Middlebury, that combined the picturesque with the sobriety of old Connecticut tradition.

The Constitution State may be home to some of the most affluent families in America. Some of Connecticut's houses may be very grand indeed. But Connecticut isn't showy. The Connecticut style is one of stately informality. We see it in colonial times, we see it at the turn of the 20th century, and we see it in the best of the state's domestic architecture of the 21st century.

Included in the following pages are a number of house designs taken from the Wadia portfolio that highlight the diverse and eclectic range of residential styles found in Connecticut today.

WADIA ASSOCIATES
RESIDENTIAL ARCHITECTURE OF DISTINCTION

ELIZABETHAN MANOR HOUSE

LIKE ITS CONTEMPORARY, the French Chateau style, the Elizabethan manor house of England bore a combination of Gothic and Renaissance elements that together yielded something entirely its own. As seen here, the style is identified by the windows comprising many small panes in groupings, set off by stone mullions, the half timbering, a variegated skyline of profuse gables, high chimneys, a tower with a curvilinear roof, sloping roofs, finials, crenellated parapets, and ogival arches. The Elizabethan or Tudor style has been enormously popular in American suburbia since the 1880s when it was one of the signature styles of the grand houses of Tuxedo Park, New York.

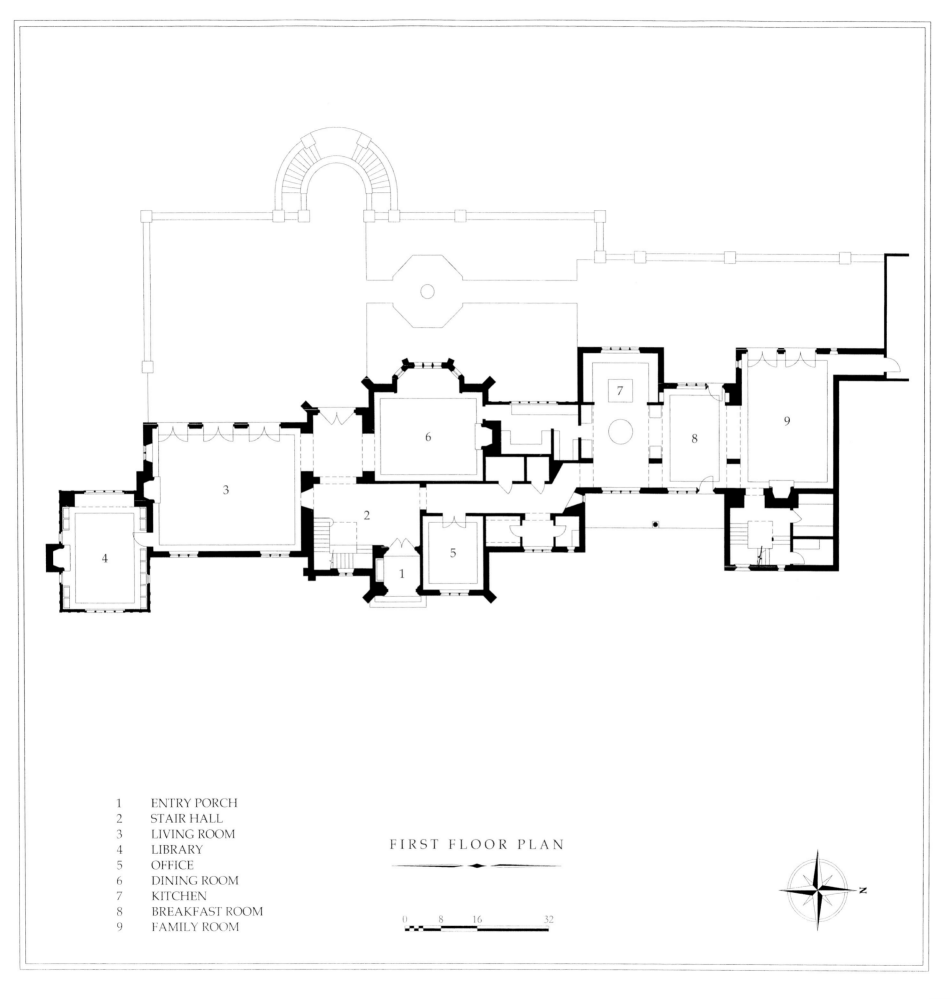

1   ENTRY PORCH
2   STAIR HALL
3   LIVING ROOM
4   LIBRARY
5   OFFICE
6   DINING ROOM
7   KITCHEN
8   BREAKFAST ROOM
9   FAMILY ROOM

FIRST FLOOR PLAN

0   8   16   32

N

FRENCH COUNTRY HOUSE

THIS FRENCH COUNTRY HOUSE is of a type designed by architects who had studied at the Ecole des Beaux-Arts in Paris in the late 19th or early 20th centuries. It comprises elements drawn from different periods of French classical architecture, assembled with High Renaissance sobriety. The quoining, mansard roof, style of dormers (with segmental-arched windows and hoods), chimneys, shutters, multi-paned windows, and arcaded entryway recall the period of Henri IV in the early 17th century. The triangular pediment and the extensive use of segmental-arched windows are reminiscent of the late 17th century, the age of Louis XIV. The use of segmental arches and balustrades also recalls architecture of the mid-18th century, such as at the Place de la Carriere in Nancy.

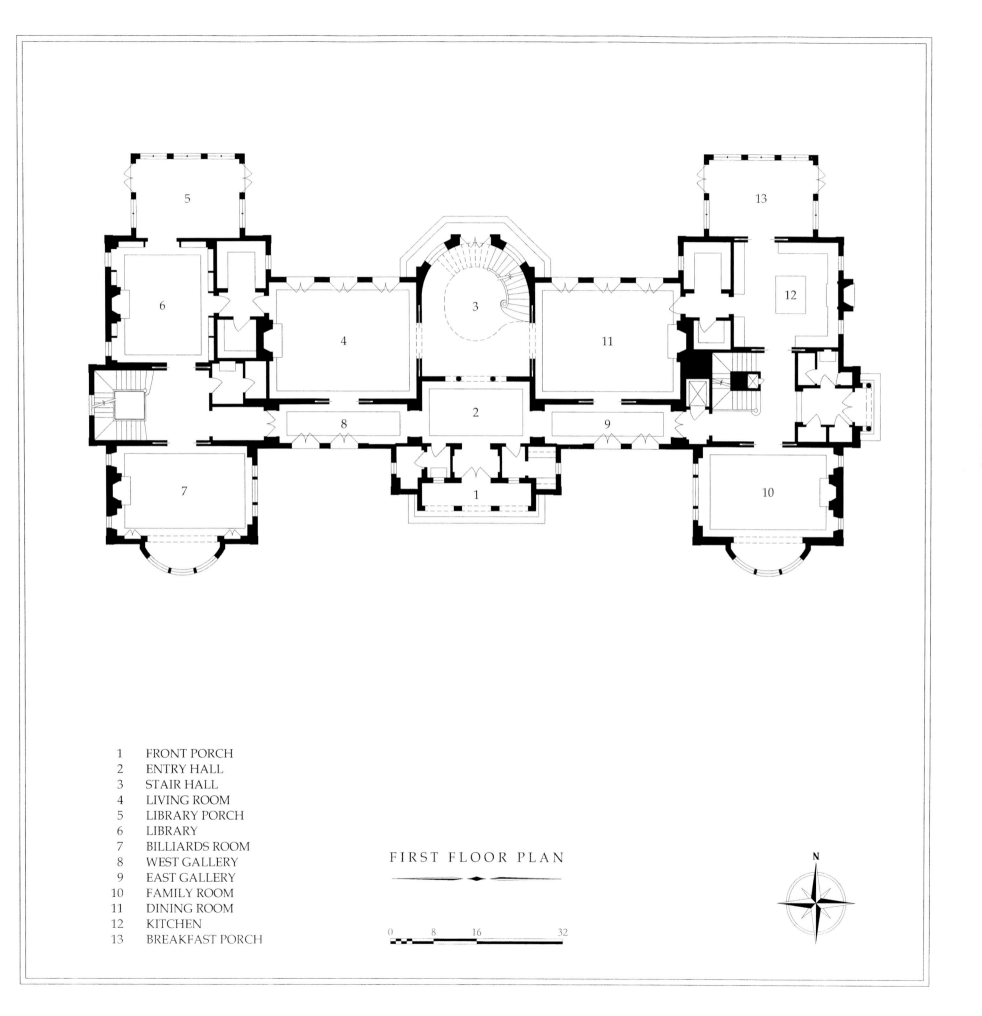

1   FRONT PORCH
2   ENTRY HALL
3   STAIR HALL
4   LIVING ROOM
5   LIBRARY PORCH
6   LIBRARY
7   BILLIARDS ROOM
8   WEST GALLERY
9   EAST GALLERY
10 FAMILY ROOM
11 DINING ROOM
12 KITCHEN
13 BREAKFAST PORCH

FIRST FLOOR PLAN

0   8   16   32

N

EARLY AMERICAN ECLECTIC

THIS STYLE IS BASICALLY 18th-century Georgian. The main block of the house is studiously symmetrical, with a hipped Spanish clay tile roof, central dormer, shutters, and a columned and balustraded double porch. The treatment of the entryway is in the Federal style: the slender columns of the porch frame an elegant doorway composed of a six-paneled door, a delicately leaded semi-elliptical fanlight, and slender sidelights. From this well-ordered block, the house grows to the left, with a façade dominated by a chimney stack faced in the same rough stone as the whole lower part of the house, introducing a note of rambling casualness such as we find with the Shingle style.

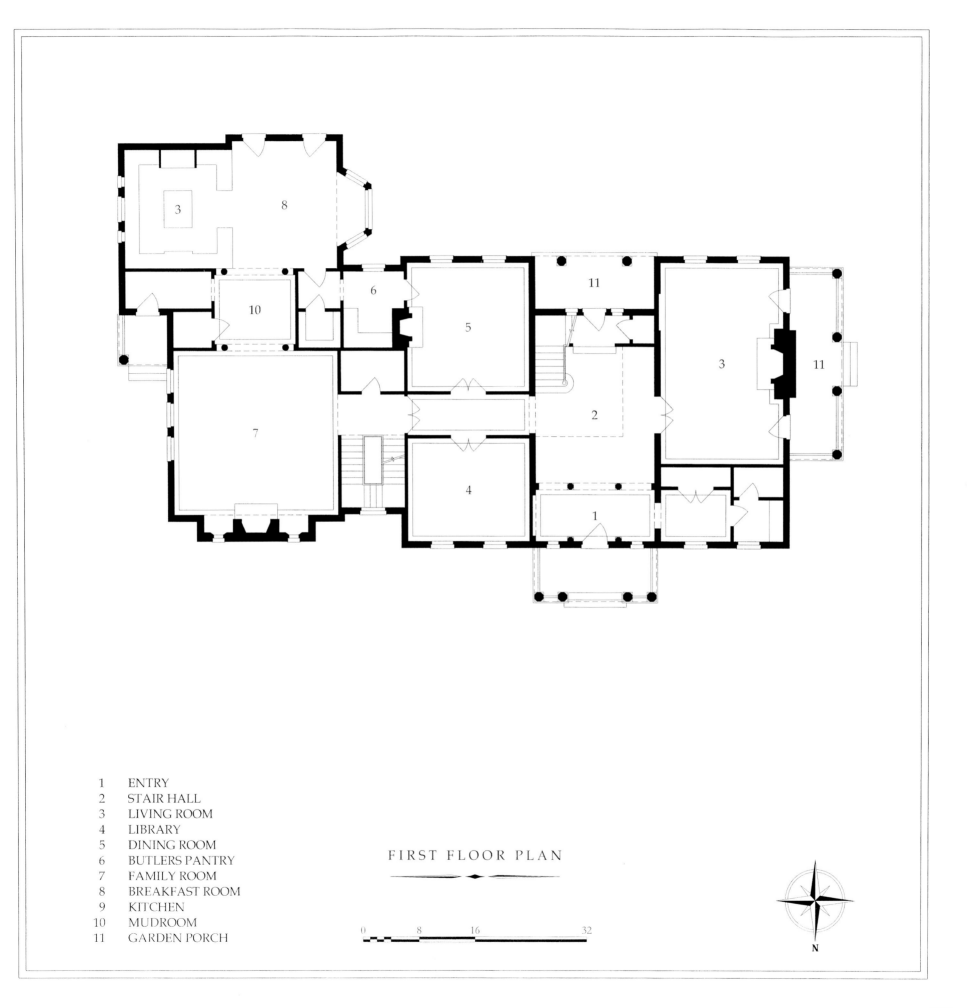

1   ENTRY
2   STAIR HALL
3   LIVING ROOM
4   LIBRARY
5   DINING ROOM
6   BUTLERS PANTRY
7   FAMILY ROOM
8   BREAKFAST ROOM
9   KITCHEN
10   MUDROOM
11   GARDEN PORCH

FIRST FLOOR PLAN

0   8   16   32

N

COLONIAL REVIVAL HOUSE

THE COLONIAL REVIVAL gained great impetus from the Centennial Exposition in Philadelphia in 1876, when all things pertaining to the nation's colonial era became objects of fascination. The architects McKim, Mead & White were simultaneously looking for a new style that would end the stylistic free-for-all of the Victorian era, be recognizably American, and offer a lightness and gracefulness lacking in ponderous mansions and city brownstones. They found their answer in columned porticos, hipped roofs, six-over-six windows, molded lintels, Palladian windows, elliptical windows, dormers, symmetrical massing, and a delicate touch, exemplified by beautifully turned slender balusters that do so much to provide the house's rhythms.

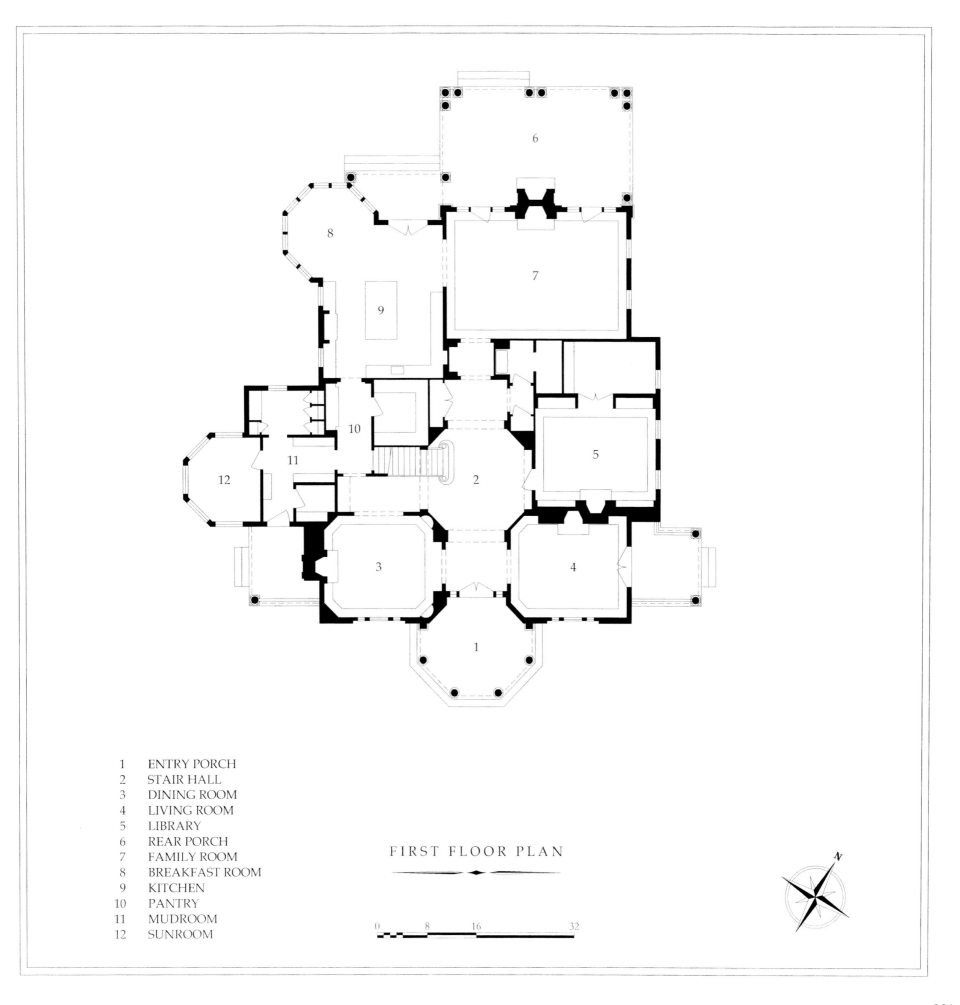

1   ENTRY PORCH
2   STAIR HALL
3   DINING ROOM
4   LIVING ROOM
5   LIBRARY
6   REAR PORCH
7   FAMILY ROOM
8   BREAKFAST ROOM
9   KITCHEN
10   PANTRY
11   MUDROOM
12   SUNROOM

FIRST FLOOR PLAN

0   8   16   32

N

FRENCH PROVINCIAL CHATEAU

THE CHATEAUX OF THE LOIRE VALLEY IN FRANCE, with their romantic sumptuousness, were a favorite of wealthy Americans in the late 19th century. Richard Morris Hunt is said to have introduced the Chateau style to New York in his house for William K. Vanderbilt in the early 1880s. But Connecticut may owe bragging rights to the style: Detlef Lienau's 1860s Lockwood house in South Norwalk was likely the first house in America to introduce Chateau-esque elements. Identifying elements include the all-masonry façades, and the picturesque skyline—where there are towers, high chimneys, many styles of dormers, and most interesting of all high, steep sweeping hipped-roofs. While the main block is symmetrical in plan, add-on parts create a casual ensemble.

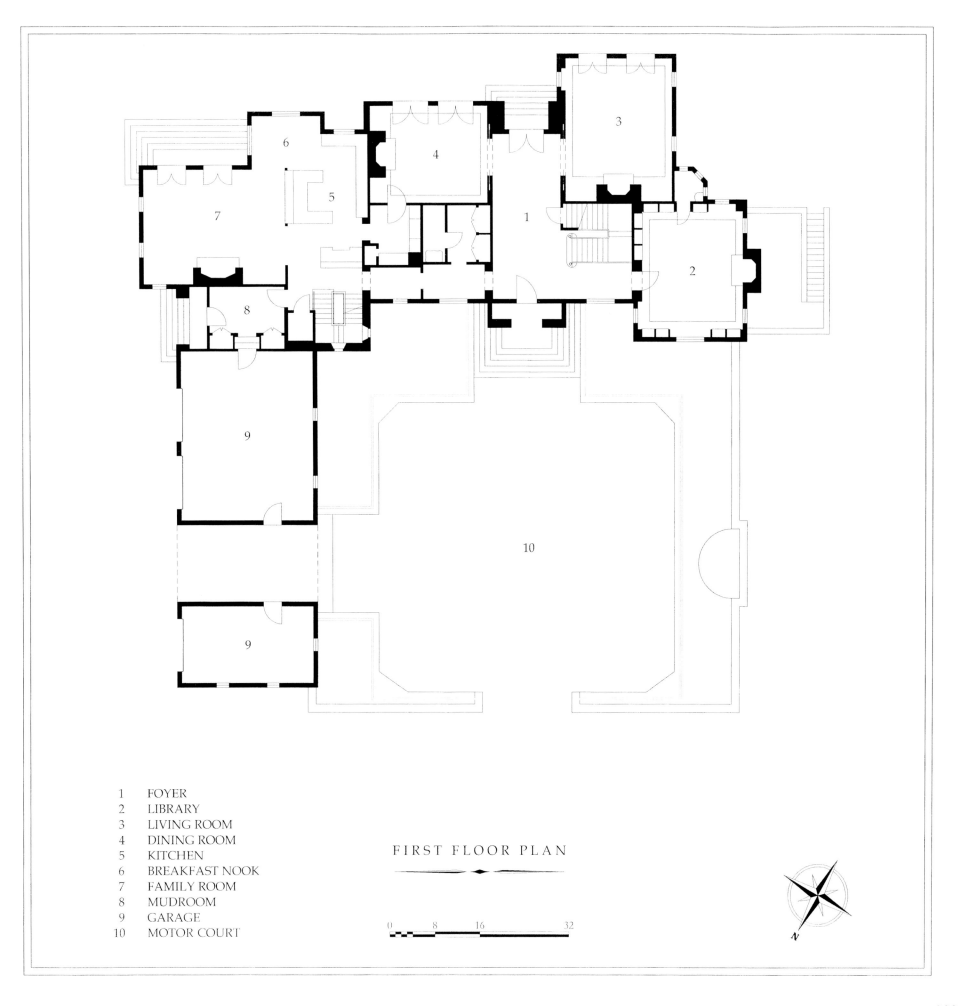

1 FOYER
2 LIBRARY
3 LIVING ROOM
4 DINING ROOM
5 KITCHEN
6 BREAKFAST NOOK
7 FAMILY ROOM
8 MUDROOM
9 GARAGE
10 MOTOR COURT

FIRST FLOOR PLAN

0   8   16   32

N

AMERICAN PALLADIAN HOUSE

IN THE EARLY 18TH CENTURY the growing interest in the work of the Italian Renaissance master Andrea Palladio brought an end to England's fascination with Baroque architecture—a trend that then made its way to the colonies. The Palladian style is identifiable here by the strict geometric massing, the triangular pediment articulated at its angles by finials, and by the eponymous Palladian window, where a high arched window is flanked by lower, square-headed windows. The hipped roof, rooftop balustrades, and especially the elaborate scrolled pediment over the front doorway are elements often found in American Palladian designs, though they were holdovers from the earlier Wren style. Such decorative pediments were common on substantial New England and Virginia houses in the period from 1730 to 1760.

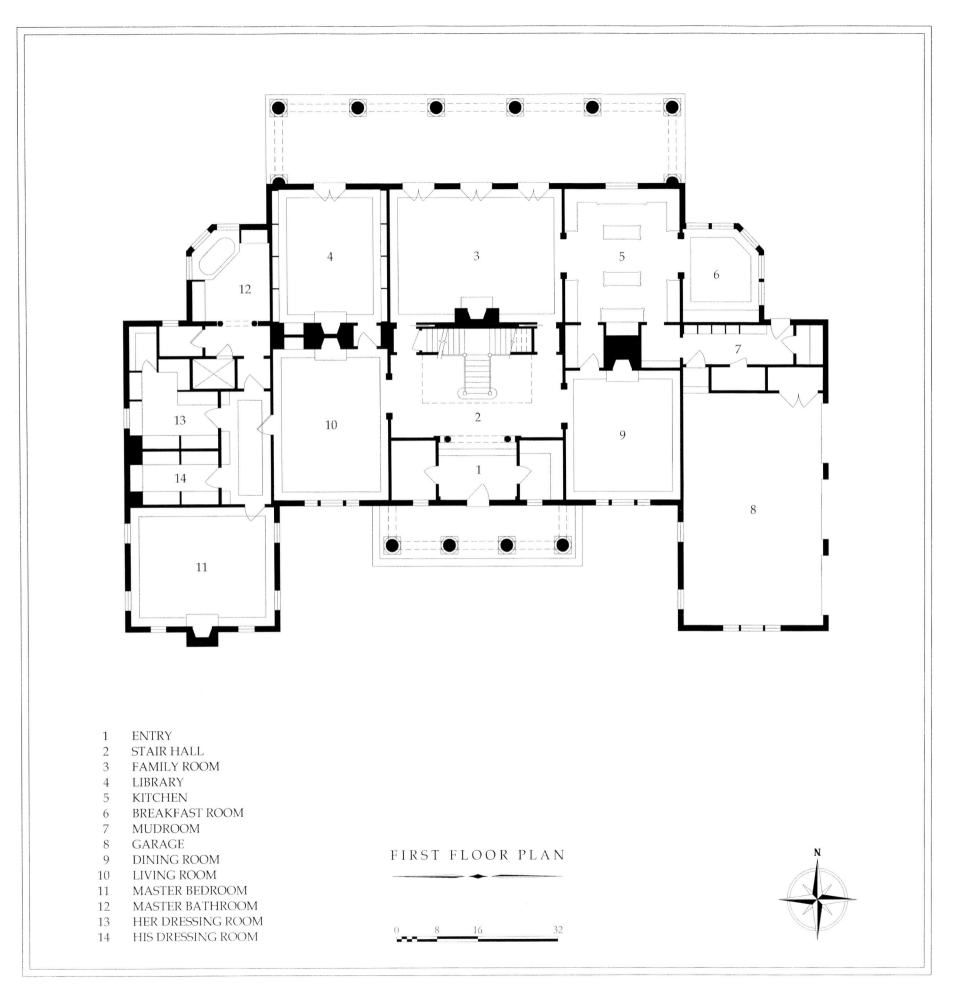

1 ENTRY
2 STAIR HALL
3 FAMILY ROOM
4 LIBRARY
5 KITCHEN
6 BREAKFAST ROOM
7 MUDROOM
8 GARAGE
9 DINING ROOM
10 LIVING ROOM
11 MASTER BEDROOM
12 MASTER BATHROOM
13 HER DRESSING ROOM
14 HIS DRESSING ROOM

FIRST FLOOR PLAN

0   8   16   32

N

SHINGLE STYLE HOUSE

IT IS NO SURPRISE WHY THE SHINGLE STYLE is called just that: shingles cover either the whole house or the upper half of the house. The casual rusticity was conceived as a natural outgrowth of old New England tradition and an Americanization of the English Queen Anne, which in its willful picturesqueness often seems contrived in a way Shingle style houses never do. Other features of the style can include columned porches, balustrades, small-paned windows, elliptical windows, and Palladian motifs, which show the relation of the Shingle style to its contemporary—the Colonial Revival style. Also typical are the complexly intersecting lines of gabled roofs, casually asymmetrical massing, and overhanging eaves. The first Shingle style house is said to have been designed by William Ralph Emerson in Maine in 1879, and such well-known architects as Henry Hobson Richardson, Peabody & Stearns, and McKim, Mead & White made special use of the style.

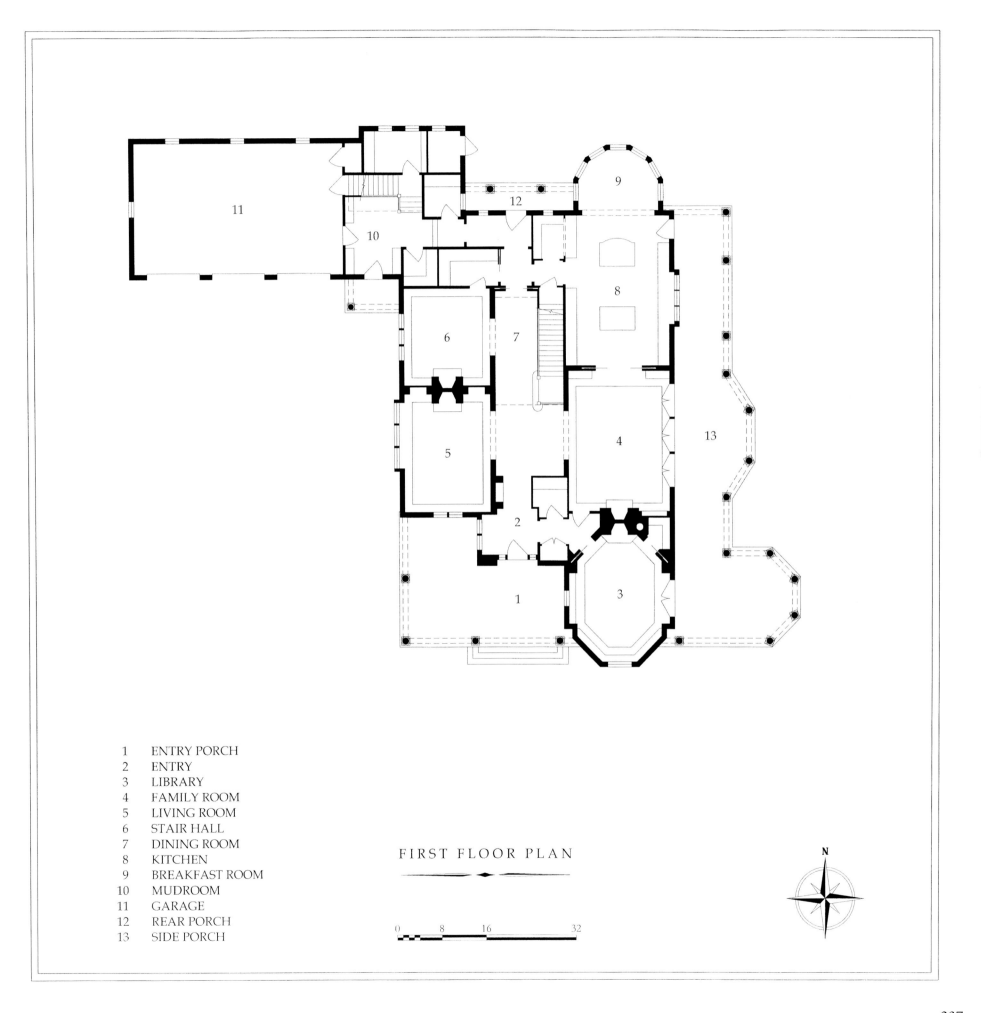

1 ENTRY PORCH
2 ENTRY
3 LIBRARY
4 FAMILY ROOM
5 LIVING ROOM
6 STAIR HALL
7 DINING ROOM
8 KITCHEN
9 BREAKFAST ROOM
10 MUDROOM
11 GARAGE
12 REAR PORCH
13 SIDE PORCH

FIRST FLOOR PLAN

0   8   16   32

N

MID-GEORGIAN FARMHOUSE

THIS HOUSE DERIVES ITS FORMS from 18th-century New England houses. The central pediment with raking cornices, the semi-elliptical window framed by the chimneys, the hipped roof, and the 12-paned windows with shutters are of a mid-18th-century type that evokes the pattern books of English architects such as James Gibbs, in which the pre-Georgian house type developed by Sir Christopher Wren is tempered by the slow introduction of Palladian elements. A feature of this house that is characteristic of New England coastal town houses of the late 18th century is the pedimented entry pavilion, first seen perhaps in the Lee mansion of 1768 in Marblehead, Massachusetts. This projecting columned entrance with a full entablature lends a restrained monumentality to the façade, and works best, as here, when it is given sufficient space to appear natural and unforced. The placement of the windows within wall arches is a feature commonly found in work of the late 18th century.

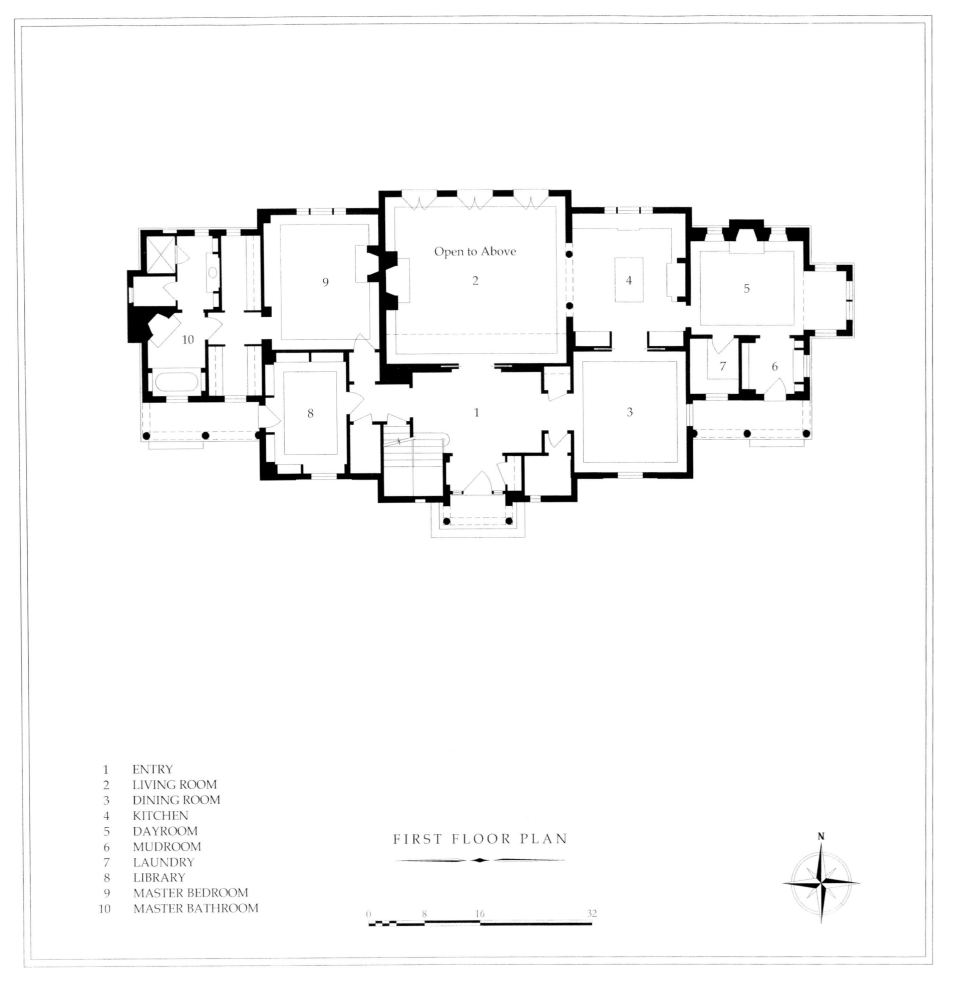

1   ENTRY
2   LIVING ROOM
3   DINING ROOM
4   KITCHEN
5   DAYROOM
6   MUDROOM
7   LAUNDRY
8   LIBRARY
9   MASTER BEDROOM
10 MASTER BATHROOM

FIRST FLOOR PLAN

0   8   16   32

APPENDIX

FIRM PROFILE

THE OFFICES OF WADIA ASSOCIATES

LIST OF PROJECTS

IN APPRECIATION

BOOK CREDITS

WADIA ASSOCIATES
RESIDENTIAL ARCHITECTURE OF DISTINCTION

FIRM PROFILE
& PHILOSOPHY

SINCE STARTING WADIA ASSOCIATES more than 30 years ago, Dinyar Wadia has earned a reputation for designing and building quality high-end homes, gardens, and interiors. Over the years, he and his experienced design team have helped sculpt the local environment— becoming an important regional proponent of Classicism, and creating traditional style homes that seamlessly fit into the eclectic fabric of Fairfield County.

Although most of the firm's work is located in the historic Connecticut towns of Greenwich and New Canaan, it has untaken projects as far afield as Chicago, California, Ohio, Rhode Island, and Vermont.

The work of the Wadia design team has been featured in *Architectural Digest, Connecticut Cottages & Gardens, Dream Homes of Metro New York, Greenwich Magazine, Modern Estate, Panache, The New 100 Houses, Veranda* and *The Classicist*, published by the Institute of Classical Architecture & Classical America.

With offices in New Canaan, Connecticut, Wadia Associates now has a staff of eight architectural designers, an interior decorator, four construction managers, and several support staff. By creating this small yet dedicated and talented design team, Wadia is able to maintain a direct hands-on approach with every project.

For Wadia, designing a home is a process of discovery and begins with a period of gathering information, most importantly about the client, but also about the site chosen to build on. Some clients may already know what they want their house to look like. Others may have a general sense based upon places they have visited or photographs they have seen. Wadia explains, "The most important thing is for a client to imagine the way in which the style of their house will complement their lifestyle—to think of the statement that they wish to make. As designers we interpret our clients' style, along with their program, and tailor it into a finished traditional architectural theme—whether that be Georgian, Colonial, or Shingle."

This personal understanding of, and bonding with, clients results in each home being perfectly tailored to express their individual needs and aspirations. It also helps explain why Wadia has so successfully achieved such a wide-ranging, eclectic, and diversified portfolio of traditional built work, as witnessed in these pages. As each individual client differs in their personal tastes, needs, and aspirations, it therefore follows that no two homes should be alike.

Although an avowed New Classicist, Wadia's pluralistic approach to traditional design is not rooted in a slavish imitation of the past. More appropriately, it is based upon reinterpreting the past and updating it for the present. And while all their designs feature the classic proportions and exquisite details of houses from a bygone age, Wadia and his team are still able to incorporate all the amenities and needs of a modern American family. As he is fond of saying, "It is traditional architecture for the modern world."

* * * * *

Wadia Associates offers the following professional services:

Residential design for new homes, additions and renovations
Interior design and decoration
Garden design
Project management and construction management

Page 240: *The offices of Wadia Associates feature hand-crafted wood Greek Doric columns.*

Above: *The second-floor gallery at the offices of Wadia Associates is suggestive of the peristyle of a Greek temple.*

An example of exterior construction drawings produced by Wadia.

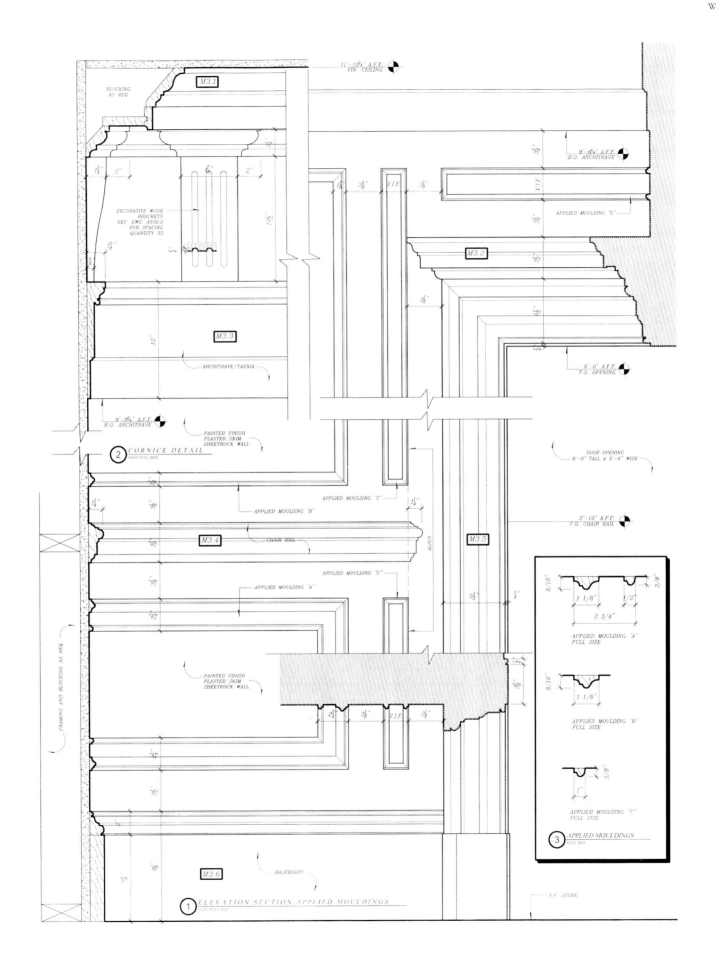

An example of interior construction drawings produced by Wadia.

THE OFFICES OF WADIA ASSOCIATES

New Canaan, Connecticut

WITH HIS PURCHASE OF A THREE-STORY, early 20th-century commercial building a few doors down from his former office, Wadia gained the square footage he desperately needed for office space and a proper library for his extensive collection of architectural books. One of the key design considerations for this new office, given the amount of time he spends at work, was that it had to have a warm residential interior. Yet Wadia also recognized the need for a modern commercial workspace. The result is an imaginative marriage of function and form. The library is designed to be the heart of the office around which the reception area, conference room, design studio, and stair hall are situated. Naturally illuminated by a skylit atrium through an open vaulted ceiling, the library exudes a wonderful sense of warmth, which is enhanced by book-lined shelves, inviting wood paneling, and a cozy sitting area.

The floor plan of the office was inspired by the layout of Heathcote, Sir Edwin Lutyens' masterpiece of classical architecture near Ilkley in Yorkshire, England. The journey from one space to another is tightly controlled to force the viewer to experience a sequence of spatial contrasts, forced perspectives, and eventual surprises. As one ventures from the reception area through the library and then to the rooms beyond, the scale of the spaces changes from intimate to expansive as the ceilings give way from single- to double-height. Capitalizing on the forced vantage points, Wadia put the many home models, photos, and renderings from the firm's projects on prominent display at every turn along the way.

Wadia designed the second floor of his office as a gallery with fluted Greek Doric columns framing the skylit atrium. The design is suggestive of the peristyle of a Greek temple. Enhancing the drama of the soaring space are two bridges, which were inspired by the industrial buildings drawn by the renowned Prussian architect Karl Friedrich Schinkel (1781–1841). The tension wires that form the sides of the bridges, which span the design studio below, are both functional and ornamental. On the principal staircase leading to the third floor, each of the balusters is adorned with a handcrafted calla lily fashioned from bronze. That no two are alike is just one of the many carefully considered details in Wadia's new home away from home.

Opposite: *A design rendering of the renovated exterior of the building.*

Above: *The skylit atrium provides natural light to the double-height architectural library below.*

The reception area, inspired by the architecture of Sir John Soane, includes a groin vaulted ceiling.

The volumetric space of the drawing office was inspired by the "Carceri" etchings of Giovanni Battista Piranesi.

Above: *Details of the millwork in the library and gallery.*

Below: *Details of the custom-designed bronze and mahogany staircases that include balusters adorned with a handcrafted bronze calla lily.*

One of the work stations in the drawing office.

PROJECT CREDITS

*Faux-painted marble columns frame the view through the living room to
Long Island Sound beyond (see pages 96–109).*

OLD MEETS NEW DISCREETLY
Pages 20–35
Design Team: *Dinyar Wadia, David Barham, Herve Hamon*
Construction Manager: *Peter Ferraro (Wadia Construction)*

QUEEN ANNE SPLENDOR
ON LONG ISLAND SOUND
Pages 36–51
Design Team: *Dinyar Wadia, David Barham, Michael Lobuglio*
Construction Manager: *Peter Ferraro (Wadia Construction)*
Decorator: *Jennifer Garrigues (Jennifer Garrigues Inc.)*

GITANJALI
Pages 52–71
Design Team: *Dinyar Wadia, Robert Butscher*
Construction Managers: *Howard Soderberg, Peter Tringali (Wadia Construction)*
Color Consultant: *Donald Kaufman (Donald Kaufman Color Formulations)*
Landscape Design: *Wadia Associates*
Gardens: *Alastair Gunn (Wadia Associates),
Joe Eck & Wayne Winterowd (North Hill Garden Design)*

A GEORGIAN COUNTRY ESTATE
Pages 72–95
Design Team: *Dinyar Wadia, Robert Butscher, David Dunn, Tony Kastor, Rick O'Leary*
Construction Manager: *Hossien Kazemi (Wadia Construction)*
Decorator: *Linda Ruderman (Linda Ruderman Interiors)*
Landscape Design: *Wadia Associates*
Gardens: *Joe Eck & Wayne Winterowd (North Hill Garden Design)*

WATERFRONT ELEGANCE
HOME TO A TREASURED COLLECTION
Pages 96–109
Design Team: *Dinyar Wadia, Robert Butscher, Katya Kopaskie, Wanda Kopec*
Construction Managers: *Hossien Kazemi, Peter Ferraro (Wadia Construction)*
Decorators: *James Petersen (Wadia Associates), Audrey Morgan (Audrey Morgan Interiors)*
Landscape Design: *Wadia Associates*
Gardens: *Joe Eck & Wayne Winterowd (North Hill Garden Design)*

CLASSIC SHINGLE STYLE BEAUTY
Pages 110–123
Design Team: *Dinyar Wadia, Robert Butscher, Wanda Kopec*
Construction Manager: *Hossien Kazemi (Wadia Construction)*
Color Consultant: *Donald Kaufman (Donald Kaufman Color Formulations)*

FRENCH CHARM
IN BACK-COUNTRY GREENWICH
Pages 124–145
Design Team: *Dinyar Wadia, Cliff Angstadt, David Barham, Fred Good,*
Construction Managers: *Hossien Kazemi, Warren Wilson (Wadia Construction)*
Landscape Design: *Wadia Associates*
Gardens: *Joe Eck & Wayne Winterowd (North Hill Garden Design)*

A GEORGIAN CLASSIC
WITH A MODERN TWIST
Pages 146–151
Design Team: *Dinyar Wadia, Phillip Dodd, Robert Lominski, Tony Kastor*
Construction Manager: *Peter Ferraro (Wadia Construction)*
Decorator: *James Petersen (Wadia Associates)*

IN APPRECIATION
It has been a long journey, and I am in the debt of many …

I thank Joel Slocum, the Foreign Student Advisor at Columbia University, without whose help I would not have been able to embark upon this wonderful journey. Joel's encouragement and perseverance were instrumental in my receiving the scholarship that enabled me to travel to the United States, and attend graduate school at Columbia.

I wish to also thank my old professor at Columbia, and mentor, Victor Christ-Janer for taking a chance on me and inviting me to work and live in New Canaan—a decision that changed my life completely. Victor's sink or swim attitude instilled in me a deep desire not only to succeed, but also to create beautiful and thoughtful designs that are the backdrop for everyday life. I thank Victor for his friendship and the confidence he has shown in me over the years.

Looking back, I owe a special debt of gratitude to my friend Roger Halle for the sound advice he gave me many years ago. At a time when I was at a crossroads in my life and ready to move to Bermuda to participate in its urban master plan, Roger encouraged me to stay in New Canaan and start my own company. Thanks to Roger, I no longer have a job, but rather an enjoyable labor of love.

To my good friends the Pascarellas and Gandhis, I thank you for your kindness and never-ending support through good times and bad.

I wish to extend my sincere thanks to all my clients from over the years, for extending me their trust and confidence. I have been truly blessed with clients whom I am now proud to call friends. I only wish that we had the space in this monograph to showcase every home that we have designed over the years. To those clients who are featured in this monograph, I am in their debt for graciously allowing us access to photograph their beautiful homes.

The beauty of practicing architecture is that it is an inclusive experience—an adventure shared with others. I have had the good fortune over the years to have a number of dedicated and talented people work with me in our office. Without their efforts and contributions the work featured in this monograph could not have been realized. I wish to thank:

Clifford Angstadt	David Dunn	Shweta Jhangiani	Robert Lominski	Martin Smith
David Barham	Peter Ferraro	Tony Kastor	Katie Maskell	Sara Stover
Tanaz Warren	Ruhshad Gandhi	Hossien Kazemi	Eric Meyer	Lee Sutch
Robert Butscher	Fred Good	Katya Kopaskie	Rick O'Leary	Peter Tringali
Stephen Davis	Alastair Gunn	Wanda Kopec	James Petersen	Jeff Vollmer
Gulestan Deboo	Carol Haber	Patty Lerner	David Preusch	Lindsey Warren
Lee Deppen	Avery Hamilton	Jesse Lewis	Farzan Saleem	Warren Wilson
Phillip Dodd	Herve Hamon	Michael Lobuglio	Howard Soderberg	

In particular, I wish to thank David Barham, Robert Butscher, Gulestan Deboo, Hossien Kazemi, and Peter Ferraro—all of whom have collaborated with me for more years than I care to remember, and have been the foundation that the office has been built upon. This office could not have excelled without you.

I continue to have the greatest admiration and appreciation for all the master craftsmen whose skill, taste, and ingenuity are so evident in the projects featured within these pages. I am in debt to you all for executing our designs so skillfully and diligently.

Our design philosophy strives to emphasize the integral relationship between a house, its interiors, and the surrounding landscape. For helping to successfully achieve this goal, I thank all the decorators, interior designers, landscape architects, and gardeners with whom we have collaborated. I am in debt to you all.

I was fortunate enough to be brought up in a loving family, in an environment where I was encouraged to chase my dreams. From the onset, my mother instilled in me a deep understanding of design and all things beautiful. I often look back upon the advice she gave me—while at times I reminisce that my father wanted me to become a doctor, and wonder what if? Your memory is always with me.

Special appreciation is, of course, given to Gool, my better half, for her unending and unconditional support. None of my success could have been achieved without your love.

BOOK CREDITS

First, I would like to thank all the people at The Images Publishing Group for inviting us to be part of such a seminal book series —in particular Paul Latham, Alessina Brooks, and Robyn Beaver for making this process as enjoyable as it has been.

Special thanks is of course reserved for H.R.H. The Prince of Wales for providing the Foreword. As a both a Classicist, and a member of the British Commonwealth, it fills me with the utmost pride and joy to have him comment on our work. H.R.H. has long been a champion of classical and traditional design, and his kind words of encouragement drive us to continually better ourselves.

I thank Paul Gunther, a person with a kindred spirit, for writing such an insightful introduction to this monograph. It is humbling to have Paul comment on our work, as he is a person highly respected among his peers, and perfectly positioned to authoritatively commentate on contemporary Classicism.

For the beautiful photography featured in these pages, I thank Jonathan Wallen and his assistant Lester Ali for their tireless efforts. Thanks is also given to Durstan Saylor, and David Sloane for their contributions.

I am also indebted to Stephen Davis, a brilliant illustrator, whose watercolor renderings perfectly capture the essence of all our designs.

For the wonderfully crafted text that so eloquently describes our work, I thank Suzanne Knutsen. I also wish to thank Francis Morrone for adding his scholarly insight to the "Pattern Book."

For their overall contributions to the production of this monograph, I wish to thank Avery Hamilton, Robert Lominski, and especially Farzan Saleem—whose tireless efforts are much appreciated. A heartfelt thanks is also given to Sara Stover, whose contribution to this endeavor—as well as to that of the office in general, is greatly and always appreciated.

And finally, a sincere thanks to Phillip Dodd for designing, editing, and coordinating this beautiful record of our work so far. Without Phillip's vision and dedication, this monograph would have remained just another unrealized idea.

* * * * *

Principal photography by Jonathan Wallen

Jonathan is a nationally recognized photographer specializing in historic buildings. His work has been featured in numerous architecture and shelter magazines. He has also been the principal photographer for the following books: *John Russell Pope: Architect of Empire*; *The Houses of McKim, Mead & White*; *The Architecture of Delano & Aldrich*; *McKim, Mead & White: Masterworks*; and *The Architecture of Warren & Wetmore*.

Project descriptions and "A Personal Story" by Suzanne Knutson

Suzanne is a freelance writer and landscape designer who lives with her husband and two children in Wilton, Connecticut. She is a frequent contributor to several lifestyle magazines in Fairfield County. Prior to founding her business, Suzanne worked as an investment banker for ten years before leaving to become a full-time mom. She holds an undergraduate degree from Georgetown University and an MBA from Harvard Business School.

Pattern book descriptions by Francis Morrone

Francis is an architectural historian, journalist, author, and teacher. He writes the weekly column "Abroad in New York" that appears each Friday in the *New York Sun*. He is the author of five books, including architectural guidebooks to New York City, Brooklyn, and Philadelphia. Francis teaches at New York University's School of Continuing & Professional Studies, and is also a Fellow at the Institute of Classical Architecture & Classical America.

Designed and edited by Phillip James Dodd

A native of England, Phillip studied at Manchester School of Architecture, and The Prince of Wales's Institute of Architecture in London, before receiving his Masters in Architecture from The University of Notre Dame. He is a Fellow of the Institute of Classical Architecture & Classical America, and is currently a residential designer in the offices of Wadia Associates.